LOOKING FOR HAPPINESS?

LOOK INSIDE!

A FAREWELL TO ANXIETY

ALBERTO VEZENDI

LOOKING FOR HAPPINESS?

LOOK INSIDE!

A FAREWELL TO ANXIETY

 Vezendi BOOKS

Can any one of you by worrying
add a single hour to your life?

Matthew 6:27

CONTENTS

INTRODUCTION

W hy squander our life – the only one we have – in a permanent state of want and anxiety when we can live a life of abundance and bliss?

Why make our happiness depend on externalities when the only truly lasting happiness is inside each one of us?

Why sacrifice the happiness we could be enjoying today on the altar of a vague promise of future bliss when we already have everything we need to be happy in the present?

Happiness is not an unattainable dream, not even a future goal we're doomed to pursue forever in vain, but a natural, innate gift we've all been endowed with. We have now, and always have had, all the happiness we'll ever have, but we don't allow it to bloom in our lives because we've unconsciously buried it under an ever-thickening layer of impediments that prevent it from manifesting every day of our life.

Our happiness is like a perennial inner light that can easily be covered and hidden, but never extinguished. It's inherent to life and will always shine, from the cradle to the grave; so once we have removed the obstacles that have suppressed it for so long, our inner happiness will shine again stronger than ever, illuminating our whole existence.

However, before we can uncover our happiness we first need to be aware of the forces that have repressed it into oblivion, as only then will we be able to fight those forces and retrieve our natural state of happiness. Which is precisely the objective of this book!

In this work, we'll learn how to recognize the two main obstacles to happiness: attachment and anxiety; and see ways to overcome them.

In the first part, we'll focus on attachment to objects and people. We'll see how attachment inevitably leads to fear, and that fear is incompatible with happiness. We'll examine the role of craving and desire, of want and satisfaction, of control and freedom, of possessions and love – and we'll see that precious little is needed to live a happy life.

In the second part, we'll delve into what is probably the main cause of unhappiness: anxiety. We'll see that most of the worry that taints our happiness is unjustified because it stems from adversities that only exist in our mind. To understand this reasoning, we'll analyze how we create all our expectations and fears in the present, how we project them into a future that is no less a product of our own imagination, and how we then await with apprehension the arrival of that future in which we have placed our hopes and misgivings.

This book is here to help you find your happiness, but to do so it has to challenge many of the received ideas and dogmas that for centuries have condemned humanity to unhappiness. Please read it with an open mind, and don't allow your conditioning to predetermine your stance towards the matters discussed within. Consider with fairness whether the ideas contained herein make any sense for you, and when doing so, be honest with yourself and don't let other people's opinions influence your conclusions. Remember that ultimately you are your only judge, and that on your deathbed the opinions other people may have about you will not change the verdict of your conscience about how you lived your own life.

Your happiness is in your own hands, and nowhere else, for only you can make it real.

Open your eyes and let the magic happen!

I. BREAK THE CHAINS OF ATTACHMENT

People make arbitrary distinctions between existence and non-existence, good and bad, right and wrong. For people, life is a succession of possessions and attachments, and then, because of this, they must assume the illusions of pain and suffering.

The Teaching of Buddha[1]

WHY ARE WE ATTACHED TO PEOPLE AND THINGS?

T he roots of all our attachment are to be found in one of the biggest misconceptions about happiness: the belief that we need *something* or *someone* in order to be happy. Such a belief makes all happiness contingent upon possessing that "thing" or "person."

From childhood, we have been conditioned by the belief that we need objects, money, people, possessions, titles, appreciation, etc. before we can be happy. To make it worse, the social environments in which we live, and especially the media, confirm and perpetuate that belief every day.

Putting it bluntly, the conditionality of happiness simply means that *you refuse to be happy* unless all the requirements for your happiness are met, which is tantamount to the effective self-denial of happiness. Firstly, because chances are that all your requirements will never be met, and, secondly, because even in the very unlikely event that you were to manage to obtain every single thing you desired, you would still not be perfectly happy because you would be afraid of losing the people or objects you believe to be the cause of your happiness.

Above I deliberately used the expression, "We refuse to be happy." Indeed, happiness is not something external that we can ever obtain and possess, but rather something that we already had at birth and still have. We all had it, and we all still have it, but we unconsciously refuse to let that happiness manifest in our lives! We repress it with all kinds of obstacles: fear, violence, hatred... and, of course, attachment and possessiveness. We place conditions on our happiness: "I refuse to be happy unless I possess that house, that car, that job, or that person," and this refusal dooms us to spend our entire lives chasing after a moving target that we will never attain, simply because our desires can never be lastingly quenched by increasing our personal and material possessions. In summary, the more we make our happiness depend upon externalities, the deeper we bury our only real and independent happiness, our inner happiness, until it can no longer manifest in our lives.

Conversely, if your happiness is *within* you, and is unconditional, you'll be happy regardless of what happens outside of you.

There is, however, an even worse side effect of attachment: fear. Attachment inevitably leads to possessiveness, possessiveness leads to jealousy, jealousy leads to fear, and fear is incompatible with true happiness. As long as the presumed source of your happiness is external to you, you'll live in permanent fear of losing your happiness. You'll only be able to control the source of your happiness if it is within you, otherwise your happiness will always depend on the wishes of other people, or on an ill twist of fate, which may deprive you of your happiness at any time. You become attached to those external factors because you assume that *they* are your happiness, and logically you want to own them forever, but deep down you know it's impossible, and so, every single moment of happiness in your life is tainted with fear.

Below we will focus on the present, on what can we do now to be aware of all our attachments, and on how to overcome them.

DETACHING OURSELVES FROM MATERIAL THINGS

Material possessions can never bring us *lasting* happiness. The more we have, the more we want, and any material possession that we mistake for our happiness simply creates in us the fear of losing it.

Let's now look in more detail at what are, in fact, two sides of the same coin: desire and fear.

DESIRE

The acquisition of new possessions, especially those that we desire, may appear to bring about happiness, at least for a while, because they distract our mind for a time after acquiring them, but in the long run they leave us feeling empty inside, longing for more, craving for something new, something better. For it's never the object itself but our unfulfilled desire to possess that object that is at the root of all craving.

Once we fulfill our desire, we start to lose interest in the object that was the very cause of that desire. As Giacomo Casanova wrote in his *Memoirs*, "Desire stems from want – we never desire what we already possess."[2]

If there were to exist any kind of direct proportional relationship between possessions and happiness, all the poor in this world would inevitably be unhappy, and all the rich would be automatically blissful, and in between, any person richer than someone else would also necessarily be happier than them.

Being rich is just a *state of mind*, though; it has nothing to do with money or possessions. Once our basic needs are fulfilled, being rich or poor, happy or unhappy, depends only on our thoughts.

Most of the happiest people I have met in my life were what society would consider "poor". I have also known people who had more money in the bank than they could ever spend even if they were to live two hundred years, yet they were miserable wrecks.

The lack of a direct correlation between the economic situation and the level of happiness of the population is one of the ironies that haunt the whole world but are more visible in some countries. Let me quote two passages from the *World Happiness Report, 2017*:

> *The central paradox of the modern American economy, as identified by Richard Easterlin (1964, 2016), is this: income per person has increased roughly three times since 1960, but measured happiness has not risen. The situation has gotten worse in recent years: per capita GDP is still rising, but happiness is now actually falling.*
>
> *In the past quarter-century, China's real GDP per capita has multiplied over five times, an unprecedented feat. [...] In the face of such new-found plenitude, one would suppose that the population's feelings of well-being would have enjoyed a similar multiplication. Yet, as will be discussed, well-being today is probably less than in 1990.[3]*

All consumer societies are based on the constant creation of needs that consumers believe they must satisfy if they ever want to be happy. However, for such systems to work there has to exist a link between possessions and happiness in the mind of the consumer, so the first step is to create and maintain that link – and the earlier the better!

Don't most advertisements portray extremely happy people wearing or using the objects that are being marketed: cars, phones, clothes, jewelry? And are not the child actors who appear in ads playing with the toys that are being advertised the happiest children in the world?

Society and the media in general are relentlessly bombarding us with messages focused on trying to make us believe that we'll be happier when we buy whatever they're trying to sell us. And since any message when repeated a sufficient number of times becomes a fact, or a truth, in our subconscious mind, we end up associating these products with an increase in happiness.

Big bright objects produce big bright smiles! Or do they? Who is happier – the hermit who is always completely satisfied with almost no possessions, or the millionaire who, in spite of all his wealth, lives in a state of permanent discontent because he craves for more?

Say you have a car that works perfectly well and is big enough for your needs, so you've no desire to have a second car or to change it for a more powerful one. In that case, you'll be focusing your thoughts on what you *have*, and not on what you *could have* or *need*. You'll be satisfied, thus creating *a reality of wealth*, and your mind will react in accordance with that perceived reality in which there is nothing lacking. You will be in "growth mode." You own just *one* car, yet you are *rich*.

On the other hand, if you own five cars, but you

still crave that supersonic sports car, or a brand-new Ferrari or Mercedes, you're not focusing on what you *have*, but on what you *don't have*, thus creating a *need*, and sending a *message of lack* to your mind. Since you cannot hold contradictory thoughts in your mind at the same time, your mind will interpret your input as one of need, regardless of how many cars you already possess, whether five or fifty. As long as you focus your thoughts on what you don't have – and there will *always* be things you don't have – you'll be doomed to live in a state of self-imposed dissatisfaction. As a result, despite owning *several* cars, you will be *poor*.

The difference lies not in the number of cars, or in the amount of possessions or wealth a person has, but in the mind of each individual. Contentment has nothing to do with material possessions. It's your subjective perception of your actual situation that determines your level of happiness and satisfaction. If you are not unconditionally happy today with what you already have, no plan, holiday, or object can make you happy... ever!

> *Future happiness is no more than a myth: don't waste your life chasing a ghost!*

In relation to this, at the very end of the Parable of the Talents we read what appears to be one of the most cryptic and controversial passages of the New

Testament:

> *Whoever has will be given more, and they will have*
> *an abundance. Whoever does not have, even what*
> *they have will be taken from them.*

Matthew 13:12[4]

These lines seem to contradict other parts of the New Testament, such as the Parable of the Rich Young Man – in which Jesus declares that it is easier for a camel to go through the eye of a needle than for a rich man to enter the Kingdom of God – and many other passages of the scripture where being poor seems to be a virtue. However, the contradiction is only apparent. Here is how I interpret these words:

In life, once you realize that there's very little you really need in order to live, once you focus on what you have instead of what you don't have, and once you tell your subconscious mind that all your needs are satisfied, you will always live in a state of abundance and thus be the "richest" person on Earth, regardless of your actual possessions. In contrast, when you see life through the prism of what you don't have, even what you do have loses its value because you only focus on your self-created unsatisfied needs and you refuse to be happy unless you get what you don't have.

The reason is that your subconscious mind controls your whole life. It determines everything you are and how you interact with the world; and your subconscious mind is always listening attentively because to perform its function it needs information about the environment. Most of that information is objectively provided by your senses, but you can alter that neutral input with the thoughts you entertain in your conscious mind. Indeed, every time you *think*, you are adding to that objective information your subjective opinion about your environment, and since your subconscious mind is non-judgmental and non-discerning, it will react to all the stimuli it receives as if they were real.

While you cannot control the output of your subconscious mind (the way it reacts to a given stimulus), you can always control the input – and you should, as that's all you need to control your life, because by choosing the input you'll also be determining the output.

Consequently, if your subjective input is one of need or lack or privation, your subjective mind will immediately accept that that is your situation, and it will not factor in your actual possessions. Instead, it will believe that you are in need because that is the mantra you keep on repeating, and it will determine your reality accordingly.

It also works the other way around: If you feed

your subconscious mind with an input of plenty and satisfaction, of having rather than one of lacking, it will create for you the reality of a rich person. You can control your subconscious mind by carefully choosing your input. The more you say, "I have," the better your reality will be; and there's always something that allows you to say, "I have," for you wouldn't be reading these lines if you didn't have the most precious gift of all: life.

Active gratefulness is one of the best ways to boost our well-being, and there are always reasons to be grateful. In relation to this, I very much like the simple truth encapsulated in the following quote, attributed to Carlos Castaneda:

> *We don't need more to be thankful for, we just need to be more thankful.*

A life of bliss is not just a nice metaphor, but a real possibility for everyone – and the good news is that living that life of bliss is in your own hands. Actually, it's in your hands only, for no one and nothing external can give you lasting happiness; only you can! One of the main teachings of this book is that you *can* change things and attain absolute happiness, but never through the acquisition of wealth and material objects, nor through the achievement of power and fame. Happiness is already within you, and that is the only place you can find it – never outside yourself.

Please note that I'm not saying we should all become reclusive desert-dwelling ascetics, fanatically shunning people and things. After all, the problem lies not in people and things, but in our believing that we *need* something or someone in order to be happy. We can, and should, enjoy what we like in life, but the moment we attach to it we're condemning ourselves to permanent dissatisfaction and unhappiness.

I thoroughly enjoy riding my snowboard and my surfboard, but I'm not unhappy when I cannot surf because the sea is flat, or when I cannot ride my snowboard because there's no snow. I love chocolate, but I refuse to make my happiness dependent on the availability of chocolate. I love many people, and I wholeheartedly enjoy their company, but I refuse to be sad when they go out of my life – even if they're gone for good. The moment you make your happiness depend on people or objects, you become their slave. Indeed, the moment you believe you cannot be happy without them is the end of love and enjoyment and the beginning of addiction.

Always remember that you are what you think. Your thoughts permeate and define your whole being, and you can only radiate what you are. As a result, when you approach life from a perspective of need and craving, others will feel that you are incomplete and that you desire something to satisfy your wants, like a hungry animal that needs to eat, and they will thus unconsciously perceive you as a threat to their own interests, or even to their own survival. On the other hand, if you feel your needs are satisfied you will unwittingly radiate abundance and generosity, and others will notice your inner satisfaction. People will feel safe around you; they will trust you and want to collaborate with you because they don't perceive you as a threat.

Finally, it is essential to realize that you'll never have all the things you desire; so, paraphrasing Bob Dylan's father's advice to his son, as well as being grateful for the things you have, be grateful for the things you don't have and don't desire. The only way to have *everything* is to crave *nothing*, for how can anyone have more than the wisdom to enjoy everything without attaching to anything?

A man is rich in proportion to the number of things he can afford to leave alone.

Henri David Thoreau[5]

To sum up, there are two ways we can lead our lives every day. One is to consistently say and think, "I need," while the other is to say and think, "I don't need." The first makes you poor, and the second makes you rich. Try it, and you'll see that this apparently minor change in mindset has the potential to usher your whole life to new levels of happiness and wellbeing.

I know this idea seems very simple, but to be able to apply it we have first to uproot the belief that our happiness depends on externalities. We have to dismiss the false assumption that people or possessions can bring us lasting happiness, and reject the fabricated image of "success" measured on the basis of the wealth and fame, which we are relentlessly bombarded with in all settings. We also have to be aware of the goals we pursue, and identify whether they are truly our own or belong to somebody else. Then we need to decide whether we want to sacrifice our happiness on the altar of other people's expectations or follow our own happiness regardless of what they may think about us. We have both the freedom and the responsibility to make that decision.

FEAR

Implicit in the belief that objects of any sort can make us happy is the idea that the loss of those objects means the loss of our happiness. Consequently, we identify the fear of being deprived of those objects with the fear of being deprived of our happiness, and due to that ever-present fear of unhappiness as a result of a loss, we develop a strong attachment to all the objects that we have mistaken for our happiness.

An ancillary effect of this process of externalization of our happiness is that we end up forgetting that true happiness only resides in what we are, and not in what we have. The projection of our happiness onto external entities turns an eternal and unlimited force (as real inner happiness is) into a perishable and limited one for this reason: As long as we keep the source of our happiness inside us it will always be there for us, and the only way anyone can ever deprive us of that happiness is by depriving us of our life; conversely, all our alleged external sources of happiness will, by definition, always be at the mercy of external factors that we cannot control, such as other people's will, events, or the unstoppable passing of time. From this flows the permanent fear of loss that tarnishes our happiness.

Properly speaking, the constant fear of losing our possessions is more a state of permanent anxiety than of fear, because in general it is not caused by the presence of imminent danger. This anxiety stems from the very act of mistaking our possessions for some kind of happiness, because even in the unlikely event that we manage to retain all the possessions we have wrongly identified with our happiness, the fear of losing them is inherent in their possession, and so it will persist for as long as we possess them and are attached to them.

In other words, the problem does not intrinsically lie in what we possess, but rather in our relationship to those possessions. Objects are just that – objects, and as such, they are neither good nor bad. It is our attachment to those objects, and the inevitable fear originating from that attachment, that turns them into obstacles to happiness. And since attachment and fear only exist in your mind, you don't have to get rid of everything you have as long as you are able to change your relationship with your belongings and detach from them. Use them and take care of them, but treat them as if they are not really yours, but as if someone has lent them to you for a while.

Enjoy everything like you enjoy the scent of the flowers or the ephemeral beauty of a butterfly, always knowing that they don't belong to you and that they will soon disappear from your life.

The only way to put an end to fear is to release the bonds of attachment in the only place where they exist: the mind; for what is attachment but a creation of the mind?

A PERSONAL STORY

I can trace back the origins of my first big lesson on detachment to the summer of 1979, when I was almost six years old. My family and I were living in our native country, Hungary, one of the so-called "soft" communist regimes of the Eastern Bloc.

One late-summer day my parents told my sisters and me to pack our stuff for a two-week-holiday "on the coast" – which for us implicitly meant the Bulgarian or Yugoslavian seaside. That very evening they packed everything into the car, and the next day we all hit the road.

After we had crossed the border my father stopped at a gas station, and told us that we were not in Yugoslavia but in Austria, that we had crossed the dividing line between Eastern and Western Europe, and that we were not going back to Hungary in two weeks, two months, or even two years. In fact, maybe we would never go back.

I don't think I fully comprehended the real significance of the news, nor its long-term implications. What I did understand, though, was the immediate effect of the change that had taken place overnight: that I would not see my house, my school, my friends, or my toys again. And it was at that moment that I suddenly realized that none of those was "mine," nor had they ever been. Even the teddy bear I held in my hand, which was the last reminder of a life that had vanished, looked different now: It was no longer *my* teddy bear, but *a* teddy bear that I loved, but which might also disappear from my life at any moment without warning.

I was probably too young to miss anything from my past life, and that attitude helped me to look forward to our new life with awe and excitement, but my youth did not prevent me from grasping the big truth underneath the surface: that one's whole life can change overnight, and that while sometimes one can do nothing to prevent it, one can always choose how to adapt to the change.

Another thing I unconsciously realized was that although I now had literally nothing I was just as happy as, or maybe even happier than, before, when I had everything. Therefore, happiness could not be in any of the things I lost, but only inside of me. Obviously, at the time I did not conceptualize in any formal way this idea of happiness as being only a product of the mind, but the dissociation between happiness and objects had nevertheless been established in my mind.

As a result, in my childhood and early teens, I had the ability to live without attachments. I had an autotelic personality and was unconditionally happy most of the time, without any specific need for anything to confirm that happiness. Of course, I did enjoy the same things as other children, such as playing with friends, going to the beach, receiving gifts... but with the difference that I was not really attached to anyone or anything. I enjoyed everything, but I craved nothing!

I enjoyed the company of other children in the present moment, without any expectation that they should be there for me tomorrow. I played with my toys as if they were borrowed and I would have to return them any time I was told to do so. And above all, I enjoyed playing, bathing and fishing on the beach, and reading books. However, I never saw anything as an entitlement, but rather as a gift of life that I could enjoy only today, not tomorrow. I lived every day fully as if it was the last day of my existence, I gave myself entirely to the people around me as if I would never see them again, and I enjoyed life thoroughly without fear.

In my mind, the whole Universe had the lifespan of a butterfly, and "tomorrow" was just another word for "never." As a result, I burnt all my energy every day. I somehow *knew* that the joy of the present moment was never to return, and so, I chose to live all of my eternity in one minute, instead of dosing it out throughout a lifetime of installments.

Above all, I felt that I had nothing to lose but life itself, and waiting for tomorrow was clearly the best way to waste my life. This awareness gave me the key to making my happiness unconditional: a total absence of fear.

I'm convinced that the wisdom that helped me remain myself, independent from people and things all through my childhood, came from that first experience of loss – a wisdom that, alas, I lost somewhere along the road in my early twenties, when I became anorexic and sunk into a daymare that lasted 5 long years. It then took me almost another ten years to recover that wisdom, but that's a long story – so long that I devoted my first book to it.

Now, let's get back to the seventies. After short stays in different places, our journey in 1979 took us all the way to Asturias, on the Northwestern coast of Spain, where we finally settled down, but every summer we would travel around Spain, France and Italy, all the way to Yugoslavia, in our old Peugeot 504 wagon, the five of us sleeping inside the car. That was the part of the year I enjoyed the most; we left everything behind and traveled light as a bird – and we were free again.

Later on, in my mid-teens, I started to travel around Europe by train on my own, and just like a snail carries its home on its back, I too carried everything inside an old rucksack. I left with no plans, no route, and no particular destination. I always slept on night trains, as it was the safest and cheapest way to spend the night. I would wander about during the day, and then I would usually choose where to go next only when I arrived back at the station in the evening. If I was too tired to think I just chose a destination at random, tossing a coin or just catching the first train departing from that station. The only condition was that the journey should be long enough to last the whole night so that I could sleep on that train. I did it many years in a row, quenched the thirst for adventure that burnt in my heart, learned the equivalent of many years' worth of schooling, and never missed any of the things I had left behind.

Later on in life, after I recovered from my eating disorder – which was a spell of desperate materialism, slavery, and attachment – I deliberately chose to live a life of detachment. My life was divided between Paris, Brussels, Budapest, and Gijón. I somehow appeared to live everywhere at the same time, but the truth is that I lived nowhere. I spent most of the year traveling, and none of the apartments I occupied was "home," but rather a huge wardrobe where I would empty my backpack full of dirty clothes and fill it with clean ones.

After quite a few years on my own, I met the girl who would later become my wife, and to whom I shall always be indebted for sharing with me all the joys and hardships of a life on the road with the bare minimum for sustenance. Indeed, instead of locking ourselves up in the prison of a home, sweet home, we traveled non-stop with only a backpack each, and we spent extensive periods sleeping in tents, cars, and huts.

Only a few months after we met, we spent one summer traveling around British Columbia with just the most basic of gear, sleeping in a tent in the wonderful Canadian wilderness, and enjoying the peace of life far from the madding crowd. Then we spent another month bikepacking in Grand Teton and Yellowstone National Parks, carrying on our bikes all the gear we needed to be self-sufficient enough to sleep in our tent anywhere we wanted, or anywhere the night fell on us, including in the backcountry. This time the stuff we could bring along was limited not only by our will to travel light but also by the physical space and weight limitations imposed by our bicycles and muscles, for whatever we put on our bikes we would also have to haul with our legs all day long! In fact, after we had packed on our bikes the tent, two sleeping bags, two inflatable mats, a fishing rod, reel, and tackle, a gas stove, a gas canister, a pot, a pan, a water sterilizer, a first-aid kit, sunscreen, some basic cutlery, food, and water, there was already no room left for anything else – and we hadn't packed any clothes yet!

This experience reminded us that it only takes a minimal amount of stuff to live a happy life; indeed, if I had to describe that month in only three words, they would be: "sheer untainted bliss." I still remember a few instances of people travelling with large motorhomes who asked us to let them take a picture of my wife and me with all our gear on our bikes, to show to their friends that life on the road is possible with only a bikeload of stuff! This whole trip was one of the best proofs of how material possessions are, if anything, an obstacle to happiness – especially if you have to carry them on your back or on your bike!

After some years together we eventually got married, and then by and by decided to start a family, which happened anon, for no sooner had we made the decision to have children than my wife was pregnant, and before we knew it our first child was born. Our daughter's arrival was like Santa Claus visiting: full of presents from family and friends, so much that by the time we brought her home from hospital our house was so full of toys and baby care items that it looked like a kindergarten.

In the beginning, we did not really settle down, though, because by the time my daughter was six months old we had lived in three different countries and visited many others. However, then came a short spell of more sedentary living – short, but not short enough – because after only five months we felt trapped in a prison of things and commitments. All kinds of distractions had made us lose sight of the essentials. The three of us had been engulfed by a suffocating mass of objects, and our lives were soon ruled by mere appearances, which we mistook for reality.

We decided to get out of that maze of people and things, escape from Brussels (where we were living at that time), leave everything behind, and go somewhere to remind ourselves that we didn't need all that stuff at all – not even with an eleven-month-old baby. Our choice was, again, the Northwest coast of the United States and Canada, and the condition was to live with the minimum budget, and for each of us, including our daughter, to carry only a small bag of stuff. In all honesty, the fact that my wife was still breastfeeding our daughter did help, but even if that inexhaustible human pantry had not been available we would have still managed alright without any of the stuff we left at home. All the unnecessary heaps of infant paraphernalia that we had either acquired or received as presents remained gathering dust in Brussels, and we soon realized that all you really need to raise a happy baby is... just a baby, and a whole lot of love.

Finally – and this will be my last example – when our daughter was two years old we decided to escape from the grey Belgian winter to sun-kissed Florida, where we spent sixty-five days traveling and living in an old van. The three of us slept every single night in a cheap tent; our staple food consisted of the fish I caught and cooked in rusty fire rings; we ate on picnic tables whenever we could find one, and on the ground when we could not; and all the stuff we had with us could fit into a single suitcase. For me, those were sixty-five days in Paradise, and I believe my wife and daughter felt the same.

Recently, after telling my children an improvised bedtime story about a little star who relinquished everything she had, even her immortality, to live the ephemeral life of a shooting star, my daughter asked me which toys the little star took on that journey. I said "none," to which she retorted, "Not even her teddy bear?" Again, I said, "No, not even her teddy bear," but seeing she was disappointed, I quickly asked my daughter whether she could remember any moment in her life when she had lacked anything, and after some reflection, she replied,

"No, Daddy."

Then I asked her,

"But do you remember when we lived in a van and slept in a tent in Florida? Apart from your teddy bear, you had no toys, nothing."

She paused, as if she was trying to remember

something, and then she said.

"Yes."

"And don't you remember ever missing anything?"

"No, Daddy."

"Of course you don't, my dear. You had more toys than any other child in the world, because the whole Universe was yours! You played with seashells, crabs, starfish, pinecones, leaves, sand, stones, streams, pools, lakes, and the ocean. You held fish in your little hands, you saw more gators and raccoons than you did dogs, and you played with everything. God's entire creation was your playground, and you went for it, took it all, and played with it. You played every day with more things that you could possibly handle, but then you didn't hang on to them. Sometimes you kept one big conch here and there for the night, maybe, or one of those fragile empty horseshoe crab carapaces, but the next morning you just left them again on the sand of another windswept beach. You just let them go, because you knew the next day amazing new toys would be waiting for you, and every day you had a whole new world to discover. You had nothing, but you had everything!"

And she truly did! And we all do too! But if we want to see it, we have first to close our eyes to all attachment and be free like the wind.

When it comes to getting rid of our attachment to material belongings, though, most of us only learn it the hard way, when life deals us a hard blow and we lose everything we have. In fact, some people – myself included – only discover lasting happiness once life has forced them to accept their detachment by physically depriving them of all our possessions, only for them to realize that they did not need most of the "stuff" they had, and that not only is happiness *possible* in spite of the new situation, but it can actually be easier to attain.

Never despair when you lose out in life. Losing stuff can be one of the most liberating experiences, because when you have nothing left to lose you have nothing to fear; and when you have nothing to fear, that is where your freedom starts, and where your growth begins. A loss is never the end, but rather the beginning of a new life full of opportunities, free from the bonds of the past that tied you down, free from the heavy ballast of possessions that crushed your wings.

Remember Kris Kristofferson's words (made famous by Janis Joplin):

Freedom is just another word for nothing left to lose.

Nothing external can ever be a true source of satisfaction or happiness, for it could never be dissociated from the fear of losing it, and fear is irreconcilable with happiness. The attachment to material possessions stems from an inherent fear of losing them, and since attachment and fear are inseparable and are both incompatible with unconditional happiness, unconditional happiness can only exist in a mind that holds no feelings of attachment.

> *For where your treasure is, there your heart will be also.*

> Matthew 6:21[4]

Keep your treasure within, and it shall never fail you!

ON THE REAL VALUE OF THINGS

No object has "objective" value; the value of things exists only in our heads. Gold or diamonds have no more value than exactly what someone is ready to pay for them. If suddenly most people decided that gold and diamonds were worthless, they would totally lose their value. And, let's be honest: except gemologists and other experts, most mortals are unable to tell cubic zirconia from real diamonds – value is a creation of the mind. Furthermore, the only "quality" of such minerals is their relative scarcity. If someone could produce low-cost gold and diamonds in a laboratory, then their value would be equal to that of any mineral available in abundance, such as iron or copper.

And what about the value of money? The value of money is even more relative and conventional than that of gold and diamonds, for while the latter have some inherent utility due to their practical industrial applications, the former is totally worthless. It can, of course, be argued that the metals from which coins are made can be recycled and given a practical use, but banknotes are just dirty paper!

If you still think that these are just empty words, let me tell you a true story about the value of money:

Sometime in my childhood, while we were still living in Hungary, my grandfather gave me a boxload of old coins and banknotes and an empty album, so that I could start a collection. I still remember how my attention was immediately drawn to the never-ending series of zeros on some of the banknotes he gave me, which had face values of billions, and even trillions, of "pengő," the legal currency in Hungary during the inter-war period in the 20th century.

But how could a trillion pengő banknote ever be issued? The answer lies in the events that shook Europe in the first half of the last century.

Without going into detail about the reasons that drew Hungary into a hyperinflation conjuncture, the fact is that the incommensurate territorial and population losses suffered from the Treaty of Trianon signed in the aftermath of the First World War in June 1920 left what remained of Hungary in a direful economic, political, and social situation. In that context, among other measures taken to stabilize the economy, a new currency called "pengő" was introduced in 1927 to replace the existing currency, the highly devaluated korona. In the next fifteen years, the value of this new currency experienced some ups and downs, but in general remained more or less stable for most of the inter-war period, with steady exchange rates of approximately 5 pengő for 1 USD between 1927 and 1941. However, with the onset of the Second World War, the inflation rate began to rise rapidly, and this, together with other factors, led to a sharp depreciation of the pengő. Unsurprisingly, during and immediately after the war the inflation rate continued to grow exponentially, until in the summer of 1946 it reached the record level of ten quadrillion percent (10^{15} %), which is still the highest inflation rate ever registered in any country in the world.

In an attempt to catch up with the steady hyper-inflationary process, the Hungarian government started to issue new banknotes, increasing their face value by adding more and more zeros, so the country went from having the usual 5, 10, 20, and 50 pengő denominations, to 100, then 1,000, then 10,000, 100,000, 1 million, 1 billion, 10 billion... trillion, quadrillion... and so on all the way to July 1946, when a 100 quintillion (10^{19}) pengő banknote was issued, which is still the banknote with the highest denomination ever issued in the world! Since such long numbers were almost impossible to handle in everyday practice, two super-units were introduced to make these amounts easier to comprehend: the *milpengő* (for 1 billion pengő) and the *bilpengő* (for 1 trillion pengő). Finally, a 1-sextillion (10^{21}) pengő banknote, called *1-milliard-bilpengő*, was still printed in 1946, but was never issued as legal tender.

These interminable numbers might not mean too much in abstract, so to give the reader an idea of the real market value of the pengő, in August 1945 one kilo of bread cost 6 pengő; in November the price rose from 80 to 135 pengő; in December from 310 to 550; in January 1946 from 700 to 7,000; in May from 8,000,000 to 360,000,000; until in June 1946, people had to disburse the astronomical sum of 5,850,000,000 pengő to buy a much-craved loaf of bread!

The price of bread is a good indicator of the real value of these multi-trillion pengő notes: absolutely nothing!

You simply couldn't buy food with pengő banknotes, even if you had a truckload of them. In a country where people were suffering from hunger and deprivation the real economy was mostly based on barter: If you wanted some eggs you had to offer something useful in exchange, such as lard, milk, grain, firewood, or building materials. In fact, most essential items could only be obtained on the black market, where people would laugh in your face if you tried to trade a dirty piece of paper for something you could actually eat. In the last weeks before the introduction of a new currency, the *forint*, in August 1946, people used the pengő notes to kindle their stoves, kept them "just in case," or just threw them away...

I still keep some of the banknotes that my grandfather gave me, and I take a good look at them once in a while to remind me that the only difference between monopoly notes and real ones is that grown-ups take the latter seriously.

LAST WORDS ON MATERIAL POSSESSIONS

Although there's nothing inherently bad about money, or any other item with a purely conventional value, happiness is extremely difficult to attain unless we are fully aware that a banknote is just a piece of paper, that a diamond is no more than a piece of glass, and that a gold nugget is just a piece of metal.

Don't limit your boundless existence to any of your petty possessions – even if you are a billionaire – because the whole world is at your disposal. Use the objects you like, touch them, feel them, enjoy them as much as you can, but don't hold on to them. And don't make the mistake of thinking that these objects belong to you, because they don't. You are but a guest in this wonderful house that we call the Universe: don't be so impolite as to want to take the place of your host!

The freedom we enjoy when we learn to sever the ties that attach us to the material world is one of the most liberating experiences in life. So much so that when we manage to free ourselves from our bonds and discover how great it feels to travel light in life, there's no way back to materialism – we shun attachment as if it was the Black Death.

Behind the desires and worldly passions which the mind entertains, there abides, clear and undefiled, the fundamental and true essence of mind.

The Teaching of Buddha[1]

ATTACHMENT IN OUR RELATIONSHIPS

N ow we enter into the most important and challenging part of this chapter, in which we will examine the effects of attachment on our personal relationships.

It is important because our sentimental interactions with other people, the feelings that others elicit from us – and more specifically the love – represent one of the main sources of either happiness or unhappiness. And it is challenging because most of what you will read below is likely to be in direct contradiction to the generally accepted concept of love, and, since our mind prefers the known to the unknown, it will be reluctant to accept the validity of new interpretations of reality.

The main idea we will discuss below in detail could be condensed into the following sentence: "It takes one to love, but it takes two to fear."

IT TAKES ONE TO LOVE

It takes one to love because real love is unconditional. You do not love *because*, but *in spite of*; you love *no matter what*. The moment you say, "I love you *if*," then your love becomes conditional, and the moment you subordinate your love to the fulfillment of a number of conditions it is not love anymore; it becomes barter. True love is giving without expecting anything in return.

Here again, the problem stems from the way our societies describe love, and from how this description, repeated again and again and again, ends up overwriting our original data and conditioning our mind.

As a matter of fact, since our early childhood, we are exposed to an image of love that has nothing to do with real love. What we see in our childhood tales, in the media, in books, in traditions, in the actions of the people around us, and even in the law, is not love, but possession; and possession leads to jealousy, fear, and attachment.

On top of that, possession is the worst enemy of freedom, for both the possessor and the person we try to possess. For the latter because it makes us want to control the person we believe to be the source of our happiness with the ultimate goal of depriving them, at least partially, of their freedom.

And for the person wanting to possess because any attempt to control what by its very nature cannot be controlled is vain and doomed to failure. Only frustration and unhappiness can grow where the seeds of fear, possessiveness, and attachment have been sown.

Apart from some notable exceptions, we grow up in a social environment in which most depictions of love are strictly based on reciprocity. Since our birth, we are fed an idea of love based on the "I love you and you love me" axiom. According to this model, a perfect state of reciprocity seems to be the panacea, the ideal relationship that everybody should aim to achieve. However, since there is no way you can experience the feelings of another human being – including love – in reality, the phrase mentioned above only makes sense from a strictly personal point of view, so in practice what it really means is, "I love you, provided that I believe that you also love me." In other words, your love is totally conditional because you make it depend upon the real or perceived reciprocity you get from the person you "love."

Sometimes the idea of love can get even more distorted and result in statements such as, "I love you because you love me," or, worse, "Since I love you and I've done so many things for you, I am entitled to expect that you love me." This reasoning, in turn, leads all the way to a paradigm of overt possession which is so far removed from real love as the two poles of the Earth are from each other, and yet a paradigm that seems to be perfectly acceptable to most people. Indeed, nobody appears to be shocked at hearing statements that pervert love into liberticidal possessiveness, such as, "You are mine," or "I am yours." On the contrary, they have become so ubiquitous in the media, songs, movies, books, etc., that people just take them for granted.

However, declarations of imposed ownership or self-inflicted slavery such as the two mentioned above should repulse anyone who believes in unconditional love and freedom – even if that means going against what appears to be the mainstream opinion about love. I for one believe that any relationship based upon the "You are mine"/"I am yours" model is built upon the imposition and acceptance of sheer emotional bondage under the cover of "love." I certainly don't want anybody to be mine, and much less do I accept the obliteration of my own self by becoming somebody else's property.

The kind of relationship described above has nothing to do with love. It is rather a contract, a barter, a trade... "I give you something, and you give me something in return." It is almost like an economic consideration of the profitability of a relationship based on the analysis of its ROI: "I value my relationship according to the return on the love that I invested in it. If my love is reciprocated I will have made a profitable emotional investment, but if it is not, I will have made the wrong investment."

When the perceived value of a relationship is calculated on the basis of the degree of reciprocity between the partners, that relationship is not based on love, but on the estimated viability of a tacit commercial agreement between two parties.

In simple terms, a relationship built on the presumption of reciprocity implies that you only love when you have reason to expect something in return for the love you give. Sounds good? If it does, read on, because this confusion of love with reciprocity invariably leads to the creation of a toxic debt.

Indeed, for as long as we mistake love for a retribution that we feel bound to pay to another person, or that we feel entitled to receive from another person, we will always remain delinquent debtors and creditors, because we will never be able to fully meet the expectations of that person, nor will they ever be able to satisfy ours. In other words, any relationship based on an expectation of reciprocity is bound to be imperfect because, by definition, our expectations can never be fulfilled, nor can we ever satiate anybody else's. Just as we saw in the previous section in relation to the insatiable desire to possess more and more objects, we are here in the same situation with reciprocity-based personal relationships. When we approach love not from the perspective of giving, but from that of receiving, we are in for a permanent disappointment, for no one or nothing can ever quench our ever-growing desire to receive more and more.

On top of that, you have to ask yourself the following questions in all honesty: "Did the person you love actually ask you to love them? Was it not you who one day felt attracted to the other person without their ever asking for it?"

When you approach your relationship from the stance of believing that the mere fact that you love someone gives you the right to be automatically loved in return, you are imposing an unsolicited liability on another person that they will never be able to redeem. A system like that could work if love was a mathematical equation and all relationships were symmetrical, but that is not how our world works. The fact is that every relationship based on self-created entitlements is necessarily asymmetrical. A perfect situation of reciprocity does not exist.

Finally, even from a strictly pragmatic point of

view, we have to understand that any expectation of permanent reciprocity from another person can only be based on the belief that we can manipulate that person, which, in the long run, is impossible. Indeed, such expectation is always futile for a very simple reason: We are not the other person, and thus we have no control over their feelings, which not only *may*, but most probably *will*, change with time. Not to mention that if we are to comprehend reality as it is, and not as we have been conditioned to see it, we have to accept that when it comes to love, not only are we unable to control the feelings of another human being, but even that other person doesn't have full control over them! Nobody can force their own mind to truly love another person, so how could anyone expect to force another person to love them? It is simply impossible. Love is sovereign, and as such, any attempt to enslave it is doomed to fail – and the sooner we admit that, the healthier our relationships will be.

WILL I?

With regard to love and relationships, we cannot ignore the significance of marriage as a means of establishing a family that is recognized by the law.

To begin with, it is important to remember that marriage is no more and no less than a public contract, a social and legal act which, in spite of its importance, has nothing to do with love. At the same time, let me make clear that there is nothing wrong with marriage. So am I contradicting myself? No, I am not, for there is nothing wrong with marriage *provided* we know what it really is: a conventional agreement sanctioned by law and registered in an official document. As such, it is a very useful affidavit of the legal and social status of the spouses, which will grant them a considerable number of entitlements, as well as imposing on them some important obligations. Furthermore, it has an undeniable social role in securing society's blessing for the union of two people.

All the reasons above led my wife and me to choose to get married in order to give a formal character to our existing relationship, but we are both well aware that, beyond the sumptuous celebration, our wedlock was an official act, not much different from getting a passport, or registering the births of our children.

In summary, while official recognition of the social situation of a person does make a difference, at the end of the day it is not a birth registration that gives life to my children, nor do our passports create our identity, any more than our marriage certificate infuses love into our relationship.

When I was a teenager I wrote the following

sentence in my diary: "I do not know whether eternal love exists, but I do know that if it does, it needs no contract as a reminder of its eternity." Now, thirty years later, I still believe that this idea holds true.

No contract in the world can secure love for either of the spouses – ever. I mentioned above that love is free and sovereign, and so it is. With a contract, or with social, moral, physical and/or psychological pressure, you can force another person to live with you, to have children with you, to keep you company for a lifetime, and even to *seem* satisfied in the relationship, but you can never ever force anyone to love you. Love is a complex innate feeling determined by a myriad of individual factors, which occur frequently in isolation, but seldom simultaneously. In fact, the combination of more than a handful of them at any given moment is as rare as a black pearl, and this is what makes love unique and magical.

So am I saying that all couples should separate when the love is gone? No, I am not. Every situation is different, and often – even when the magic of love is gone – there may well remain enough of the above-mentioned factors to sustain a wonderful relationship. For instance, sexual attraction is rarely lasting, because our hormones and instincts make us unconsciously want to diversify our intimate partners, for the very compelling reason that genetic variation is the best guarantee for the survival of any species. (Naturally, our instincts predate all contraceptive methods.) In this instance, what usually happens is that passionate love grows into a sincere and deep friendship (and I don't mean "friendship" in the way *Facebook* has misappropriated this term, but *real* friends, which I, for one, can surely count on just one hand).

Did I say "grows"? Yes, because passion is inherently volatile and short-lived, but a true friendship based on respect, admiration, care, tenderness, understanding, shared interests, and a certain commonality of purpose, enhanced with still-pleasurable sexual activity is probably the best and most lasting kind of relationship between two emotionally sovereign and independent adults; one, in the end, that I would not hesitate to call *love*. And you never know – hormones sometimes behave whimsically and sexual attraction often returns… so why not give it a chance?

Furthermore, there may be other equally important reasons to stay in a relationship despite the love having partially faded away, such as having children in common. Indeed, two adults may well choose to stay together to ensure the best possible emotional environment for the development of their children. In fact, relationships of this kind can work perfectly well provided that the partners get on well and respect each other; even considering that, since most relationships are asymmetrical, a permanent intimate relationship devoid of love often requires a much larger sacrifice from one of the partners than the other. Again, it's a sacrifice that can be worth making for the sake of the children, and also for the sake of that lasting enhanced friendship that we can still call "love," but not for the sake of fear, money, religion, or social norms.

When a relationship is maintained solely out of fear, or under any kind of pressure or coercion, it only makes for two miserable people and perpetual unhappiness.

It is not righteous to live in contractual concubinage with a man or woman you no longer love just because of fear, because society expects it from you, or because you don't want to hurt your partner. As for the latter, I would be deeply troubled and humiliated if ever I learned that my wife was wasting her life with me just because she did not want to hurt me. That is compassion, or pity maybe... but not love.

Sharing your life with another person must always remain a choice, and never an obligation of any kind (moral or otherwise).

Then what about love? Well, real love is a maverick, always the result of a magic that we cannot control. It comes and goes of its own accord and there is nothing we can do about it. Enjoy it while you can, and don't waste your time trying to chain it down. Because you can't!

Let me quote from Casanova's memoirs:

> *If, when I hear some women saying that men are perfidious, and accusing them of inconstancy, I also heard them assure that these men had the intention to deceive them already when they promised an eternal constancy, I would say that they are right; but none can, because in general, when we love, we only promise what the heart dictates, and consequently, their lamentations only excite in me the compulsion to laugh.*
>
> *Alas! We love without consulting reason, and we also cease to love without her intervention.*[2]

WHO DO YOU LOVE?

So far, we have concentrated on the problem of believing that love has to be reciprocated in some way, but there is yet another problem that pervades most relationships: the misbelief that the person we love is the source of our happiness, which leads to fear and attachment, as we will see below.

With the understanding that there may be reasons to maintain a relationship destitute of love, such as those mentioned above, for the sake of clarity I will limit myself in what follows to examining personal attachment from the point of view of the mind, leaving aside all external factors, such as the interests of third parties, laws, conventions, norms, traditions, culture, religious beliefs, social expectations, etc.

To be more precise, below we shall only examine love, fear, and attachment "from within" as they are created in our mind, i.e. the way *we* conceive our relationship with the other person, and how we can change that personal inner vision to the advantage of everyone. Remember that the only thing you can ever change is your own interpretation of reality, and that you have no control over anything external to you.

We have already seen what happens in our everyday relationship with the material world when we believe that objects can make us happy: We end up associating our happiness with the possession of those objects, and, consequently, we infer and anticipate unhappiness following the dispossession of those objects.

The same happens in our relationship with the people we love: We adore their company, we enjoy their attention, and we relish the pleasure they bring into our life. So far so good, as it is completely normal to enjoy what we like, but the problem arises when we come to believe that our happiness *depends on* other people, which automatically leads us to the conclusion that they *are* our happiness. And the belief that our happiness resides in an external item – an object or a person – is inseparable from the fear of losing that item, and our happiness along with it.

The moment we believe that our happiness stems from the person we love we are bound to be miserable, because we will want to hold onto them, and the fear of losing them will inevitably bring about attachment – and this is when we utter one of the most horrible declarations of attachment: "I need you." The moment you believe that you *need* another person to be happy signifies the end of love and freedom and the beginning of fear and dependence.

Finally, when you mistake a person you love for your happiness, what you really love is not the person, the independent human being, but the pleasure, company, help, and happiness you obtain from them. In other words, you are not in love with the other person, *you are just in love with your own happiness*, which you have wrongly incarnated in the other person.

Just like the greedy landholder who only loves the benefit he reaps from his land and who does not care about the soil, which he exploits until it becomes barren, when you only love the happiness you obtain from a person, you are in love with the *product* of your relationship, and not with the *person* whom you are supposed to love.

Let me give you an example to illustrate the ideas presented above:

Imagine if my wife were to come to me tomorrow and tell me that she was leaving me. Feel free to replace "wife" with "husband, lover, mistress, daughter, son…" or any other term of your choice. The condition is that it has to be someone you love. Without entering into the countless reasons why she would want to go away, for the sake of simplicity let's only assume that she is leaving me voluntarily and willingly. In such circumstances, it is pretty safe to conclude that, whatever her precise reasons may be, they all converge on the fact that she is unhappy with me, or at least that she expects to be happier elsewhere, and basically that is why she is going away. Let's also assume that once she has left me, she will, in fact, be happier in her new life.

In this situation, I have several possible options, the most common being: to be sad, to be angry, to be indifferent, or to be happy. We shall examine each of these below, but before proceeding, I need to introduce an important caveat to what follows. For the sake of argument, I will refer to the aforementioned possibilities in isolation – i.e., as pure feelings – but I'm well aware that our human nature does not work that way. Indeed, when a relationship we have built for years comes to an end it is difficult not to feel sad, even if we have attained the state of enlightenment necessary to realize that we should rejoice in the happiness of the person we love, be it at the cost of our own loss (as we shall see presently) … but it is not impossible. My proposals below should thus be construed as an ideal state towards which I believe we should tend if we ever wish to grasp the true meaning of unconditional love. In other words, with the right mindset we can learn to make the impossible possible – or at least get as close as we can to our goal, for every step in the right direction brings forth a better understanding of the obstacles that prevent us from enjoying the full life we should all be living.

Let's return now to our example. According to the dominant concept of love in most societies, I should react with sadness and/or anger, or at the most with indifference. Happiness is not an option here because people would automatically think that I was either faking and pretending to be happy; that the separation had affected me so much that I just had gone crazy; or, worse still, that the reason why I was happy was because I did not love her in the first place.

Now, what if I told you that this mainstream conception of love is totally wrong, and that in such a situation the reaction which is most coherent with love is to feel happy? Yes, *happy*, because in spite of everything, the person you love is at last happy. And yet, how remote is this reaction from what we see around us every day, both in fiction and in reality? When confronted with this situation, the dominant view is that I should feel sad, or even angry, and seek retaliation.

Let's also not forget that all my sadness, anger or violence would be directed precisely against the person I was supposed to love just a short while ago! How absurd, and yet, how common these reactions are! And the worst of all is that in such a situation society will readily approve of the sadness, understand the anger, and even condone the violence (especially in some parts of the world).

If we delve deeper into this paradigm, we'll realize that there is a causal link between her happiness and my sadness which, although frequently taken for granted, is no less misguided and harmful.

In other words, not only do I consider her gain to be my loss, but also her happiness to be the cause of my sadness!

There are several problems with this conditioned model of loss and sadness, but I will focus on the main two: the denial of our freedom to choose how we react to external stimuli, and the inherent contradiction in feeling sad when the person we love is finally happy.

In general, the automatic association of material loss with sadness is one of the most pervasive results of the conditioning processes we have been exposed to since our birth, but the situation is even worse when it comes to love and human relationships, because in this realm that association is almost universally accepted – but it shouldn't be! Indeed, such an association is misguided, because to admit that another person can impose upon us any lasting state of mind, such as sadness, implies the negation of our most fundamental freedom, the freedom to choose how we react to events that are not under our control.

"Not being able to govern events, I govern myself,"[6] wrote Montaigne almost five hundred years ago, and my contention is that the power to govern ourselves includes the possibility of choosing to be happy in spite of everything, including the fact that a person whom we loved disappeared voluntarily from our lives. I stress *voluntarily* to make clear that we are not now considering the death or enforced disappearance of a person we love, but any situation in which they willingly leave us of their own accord (for instance, the emancipation of our children or the departure of our intimate partner in search of a better life).

This idea then leads us to the second problem mentioned above. Following on with the same example, since I can choose happiness, to me the only coherent behavior if I really love my wife is to be happy for her in her new life, precisely because she is finally happy!

I know this sounds crazy. I know this vision goes against the most fundamental principles in many societies, and for many years it clashed with mine too, until I finally realized that this is the only true expression of love, and here is why:

I realized that if I want to be my own master, and not just a robot behaving as it has been programmed to do, I have to learn to see through the mirage of appearances created by my conditioned mind, and one way to do it is to challenge all my expected behavioral patterns with questions. In this particular case, a most effective way to analyze the situation would be by asking, "Why am I sad? What exactly is the reason for my sadness?"

The only honest answers I can find to these questions are the following: "Not only am I sad in spite of my wife's happiness, but the very reason that makes me sad is the same one that makes my wife happy"; and, "The true reason I am sad is because I pity myself. I am sad because I lost what I mistook to be the source of my happiness. I am sad because to me only my lost happiness is important, and not the happiness of the other person – the person I was supposed to love."

Think about it. If I truly love her, how could I possibly be sad for my wife, a person who is now much happier than before? And this is exactly the point I'm trying to make: I, me, and myself would be sad, not my wife. Consequently, the only plausible answer is that I would be sad only for myself because I had lost a possession that gave me pleasure, cared for me, and helped me.

Despite this, most people choose the easy way of relegating the real problem into denial, just as I did in the past, but no problem can be solved until we are aware of its true nature. To avoid hurting their ego, people are reluctant to admit the true reason for their sadness, and so was I, and instead of admitting that "I am sad because I pity myself," they talk about the "sorrow for the lost love," but this is just a euphemism for the basest self-pity there is. Think about it: If you are grieving when the person you love is at last happy, what is that but egotistical self-commiseration?

The corollary of this argument is that by declaring our sadness despite the happiness of the person we love, we are confessing the uncomfortable truth that what we really loved was not the other person, but only the pleasure, help, care, and company we obtained from the relationship with that person. Consequently, what we truly mourn now is the loss of all those most agreeable benefits, rather than the new situation in which the person we loved is now.

If this is your conception of love, how could you ever be able to love your foe, who gives you nothing and means you harm?

Selfishness, possession, and self-compassion – is that really what love should be?

Just like a child who has lost her favorite toy cries and wants it back, adults suffer and want their lost happiness back!

Language should be the most powerful vehicle to express the truth, and yet it is way too often distorted by euphemisms aimed at hiding disturbing realities. However, as far as we can stretch the meaning of words, it is preposterous to argue that a statement such as "I am sad" could ever be construed as including any other person but myself. Just as the acts of the created being are independent of its creator, my pain is only mine; it does not improve anybody's situation, least of all my own. It is my sadness; my wife has nothing to do with it, I have created it, and only I can put an end to it.

And that is precisely the good news! Since *I* am sad because of *my* loss, and all that sadness is but a creation of my mind, *I* can also choose not to be sad, and rejoice instead in the happiness of my wife. That is what love should be all about!

LOVE RULES

In fact, so far, we have seen what love is not; so what *is* love, then?

Entire books have been written on the subject of love, but I believe the meaning of love can be defined in one single sentence: *Love is giving without expecting anything in return.*

The sun shines for all, and real love is like the warm sunshine the Sun radiates upon all beings on Earth without distinction of any kind. It gives life to the poor and to the rich, to the good and to the evil, to the powerful and to the powerless, to the ugly and to the beautiful, and never expects anything in return.

And if love is the sunshine, possession is a black hole, which is all about wanting, all about seeking to satisfy our insatiable ego.

It takes one to love. Love is not reciprocal. Love is an individual act of detached selflessness, not contingent upon any feature of its target, but totally independent from it, immanent in its source.

Finally, love is inexhaustible. You can never run out of it; indeed, on the contrary, the more you give, the more you have. When you dig a hole on the beach in the wet sand close to the ocean it will always fill up with water, and no matter how many times you bail it out with your bucket, it will fill up again; and the deeper you dig, the more water you will get. However, as soon as you stop digging, the walls begin to crumble into the hole, filling it up with sand, and pushing out the water. That water is love, flowing from an eternal source that will unfailingly regenerate and grow when you exploit it, and relentlessly dry up when you don't.

The perfect relationship is one in which all expectations of reciprocity are absent, one in which giving happens strictly as a result of love, and not of personal interests. True love can only come freely from within. It must be unconditional, and thus hold no expectations.

Do not expect anything, and you will never be disappointed!

In other words, when you experience real love, all you want for the people you love is for them to be happy, and not just in the way *you* think they should be happy, but how *they* decide to be happy – even if that means your losing them!

When you truly love, you do not limit yourself to the golden rule that commands you to "do unto others as *you* would have them do unto you," but to go that extra mile and "do unto others as *they* would have you do unto them"! And since your only motivation is love, and your love comes from within, you do what you do because you want to do it, so naturally, you should expect nothing in return. The ones you love don't owe you anything!

On a personal note, I lost the ability to love unconditionally somewhere in my late teens, and it took me almost fifteen years of mistakes, setbacks, and heartaches, followed by years of introspection, mindfulness, and deprogramming to realize that for two decades of my life I had never truly been in love, but that what I called "love" was, in reality, a selfish quest to satisfy my own desires.

Only when I fully comprehended that love can only manifest in the act of giving, and never in the act of receiving, did I become able to express my love in the search of happiness for others, just for the sake of love, always dissociating that feeling from any expectation of reciprocity or personal attachment to that person.

Ever since, every day is my birthday, because every day with the ones I love is a gift, a blessing of life. I enjoy their presence by my side, knowing that they owe me nothing because everything I do I do out of love, that the only reason they are with me is that they freely choose it, and that I might not see them tomorrow.

Every single day becomes a gift when you

realize that nobody in the entire world can ever be forced to truly love you, and you stop taking love for granted. When you finally overcome the delusion of reciprocity and stop creating in your mind false entitlements that will inevitably remain unmet, then you begin to enjoy every single moment with the ones you love.

Consequently, I am fully aware that everything I do for others, including my family, is not because they, or anybody else, expect it from me, or because I think I should gratify the world by behaving "as I should," but because the love I feel for them naturally prompts me to act in this way. And since I act in full liberty, I do not feel entitled to expect anything in return, and hence I consider everyone free from all debt or obligation towards me.

If one day my children decide to read this book and think about their father, the message I have for them can be condensed in a few lines:

Learn to detach from everything you are scared of losing, and all anxiety will vanish from your life, because when you have no attachments, you enjoy everything without possessing anything, and thus you have nothing to lose.

Finally, remember always that you are free, totally free; that you owe me nothing whatsoever, because whatever I did for you, I did out of love. Remember also that I will always love you no matter what, as your happiness is my happiness, whatever form your happiness takes!

ATTACHMENT AND SOCIAL CONTROL

W e have seen that no possession can make you rich and that no possession can make you happy, as being rich and being happy are just ideas created in your mind. We have also seen that when we establish a mental association between happiness and possessions, not only do we end up believing that happiness can be obtained from an external source, but also that we can be deprived of our happiness by the dispossession of that external source. This association exists only in your mind and not in reality, but precisely because this belief is in your mind, eventually you come to believe that it is real, and in turn, your mind can also be controlled by it. Beware of this dangerous vicious circle, because once you are inside it's very hard to get out of it.

All the great communicators in the history of mankind who, for a good or a bad cause, were able to influence, or even brainwash, whole nations have always spoken to the subconscious mind of the individual, rather than to their intelligence, knowledge or conscious understanding. Unfortunately, this power has too often been abused for political interests, and applied through mind-control dynamics that transformed entire societies of reasonable individuals into irrational mobs deprived of all judgment and humanity.

Mobs never lead, mobs are always led, so be yourself, and be your own leader: it's the only way to be unconditionally happy. Even if you are not perfect, just be yourself, because nobody can be like you. You are unique, and if you disappear in the attempt to be somebody else the world will lose you forever.

The ability to control the mind is a source of unlimited power, regardless of who is in control! No wonder it is so, for what is our life but the constant manifestation of what we hold in our minds? That's why all the guardians of the established social order in the world have an interest in limiting the wisdom of the population, because that is the only lasting way they have to limit our freedom.

Remember *Nineteen-Eighty-Four*? "War is peace, freedom is slavery, ignorance is strength."[7]

The premise for keeping the current social order unchanged is social control, and the premise of social control is individual and collective mind control. Social control requires limiting each member of that society's capacity to think to the barest minimum necessary to be still able to perform their role in the social machinery, while not becoming a threat to the established order. No temporal power, be it financial, religious, political, racial, caste-based, etc., can survive unless it holds fast the strings of the puppets that are subdued by it. All states, religions, political systems, corporations, clans, sects... in short, all organized structures of power need your dependence on them to thrive, because independent free thinking is the major enemy of those who want to retain the status quo, and with that, their current position of power inside of it.

> *Whatever crushes individuality is despotism, by whatever name it may be called and whether it professes to be enforcing the will of God or the injunctions of men.*
>
> John Stuart Mill[8]

However, the social control enforced by the temporal or spiritual power, by the polity or the church, represents only a minute fraction of the overall forces that aim to control every single human being. Indeed, each time I refer to the control of the individual by other people or groups of people, I am not only referring to the permanent and deliberate control exerted openly and consciously by the authorities of a country, church or any other organized entity, but also to the control exerted surreptitiously and often unconsciously over the individual by their peers by means of social pressure.

While the former originates from the desire to uphold the established order, and with that to perpetuate the power of the political, economic, or ecclesiastical ruling classes, the latter stems from the desire to maintain the established system of beliefs, customs, and traditions, and is the expression of the misguided belief held by almost all groups that, since they are in the majority, they must necessarily be right. While the former derives from a few and is shortsighted, the latter emanates from many and is as blind as a bat. And while it is relatively easy to resist the obvious, and usually rather simple, vertical power of the ruling classes – at least in free countries – it is extremely difficult to oppose the subtler, and very complex, horizontal power of the masses. Or using Machiavelli's analogy, while the former is visible, acute, and concentrated, like a localized abscess, which is easy to detect and eradicate, the latter is invisible, chronic, and pervasive, like a generalized sepsis, which is much harder to diagnose and cure.

At this point let me make clear that I'm not advocating the destruction of all existing social structures, or the rejection of all established norms: most of these rules belong to the realm of natural law and are there to protect our fundamental rights and freedoms. However, many other norms have been artificially created and imposed by groups of individuals with the sole purpose of establishing and perpetuating their alleged superiority over those whom they wish to subjugate. Not to mention that most of these fabricated "laws" are incompatible with the universally recognized fundamental rights and freedoms inherent to every human being (in particular the right to life, liberty and security of person; the right to freedom of thought, conscience, and religion; and the right to freedom of opinion and expression).

What I do defend is the liberty of every person to think and act as they deem appropriate, without any other restriction or limitation than that of respecting everybody else's fundamental rights and freedoms. Besides, paradoxically, the preservation of individual freedom is not only necessary for the realization of the full potential of every person, but also for the growth of the superstructure in which that person lives. Look around the world: States which restrict individual liberty tend to regress and will eventually collapse, while freer States tend to grow and flourish. I often think of Gandhi's inspiring words: "When I despair, I remember that all through history the way of truth and love has always won. There have been tyrants and murderers and for a time they seem invincible but, in the end, they always fall – think of it – always."

Every human being is born free – and I don't mean circumstantially free, but inherently free – however, the unyielding process of conditioning into blind dependence-based obedience gradually, but relentlessly, deprives the free child of their freedom, until they become just another cog in the system. And the more conditioned and dependent they are, the meeker they are as well!

Not only will a nation of sheep beget a government of wolves, as Edward R. Murrow said, but it will also bring about a state of social regression, for no original ideas will ever arise from a herd bleating as one.

> *A state which dwarfs its men, in order that they may be more docile instruments in its hands — even for beneficial purposes — will find that with small men no great thing can really be accomplished.*

John Stuart Mill[8]

In Aldous Huxley's *Brave New World* the less conditioned and intellectually more gifted Alphas were undoubtedly more dangerous for the system than the deeply conditioned but intellectually poor Gammas, Deltas, or Epsilons. While the former had been allowed to retain some of their free will in so far as it was necessary for the social system to work, the latter had been engineered to be slaves inherently: all their free will had been meticulously annihilated during their conditioning process, and so they zealously rejected all freedom without thinking, simply because it contradicted their programming. In Huxley's world, the lower castes simply lacked the ability to even consider that there might be something good in freedom because the tortures they had suffered right from their conception had conditioned their minds to associate disobedience with punishment, physical pain and moral suffering.

Social control, which ultimately always means the control of the individual, can manifest in several ways – more or less evident, more or less violent – but they all aim at making you accept, by persuasion or by force, that you cannot survive outside of their system, that either exclusion and ostracism will kill you indirectly, or that agents of the system will take care of you, and do you in... directly.

However, in contrast to Huxley's world, where the conditioning was indelibly etched on the mind of all social classes, we have not been engineered (at least not yet), and so, we still have the innate ability to alter our program at any moment in life, provided we first recognize all our robotic behaviors and reclaim our inborn freedom to change them. And the best way to do that is by getting rid of all our attachments, because the moment we realize the big truth behind the appearances, the moment we see that to be happy we do not need anything external, our bonds of emotional dependence on others are instantly loosened and we become free.

It is essential to understand that when our basic needs are satisfied we do not *need* anything to be happy; on the contrary, we need to break free from all the obstacles that are preventing us from living a life of unconditional bliss, and the first and foremost obstacle to this is the deception that we need people and stuff to be happy.

As a matter of fact, this deceit is the very foundation of all materialistic societies, based as it is on the inexorable imposition of hierarchical structures of power, the submission of the individual to ultra-consumerism, the proscription of all independence, the banishment of freewheelers, and, ultimately, the annihilation of the self-governing, autonomous human being.

Detachment is dangerous for the ruling establishment because detachment means independence, independence means freedom, and complete personal freedom represents a threat to all the social orders built upon the blind obedience of the individual to the will of the all-powerful religious, political and financial elites. When you find happiness within – the only unconditional and lasting form of happiness – you no longer *need* anything external to be happy, and consequently, you cannot be controlled anymore, save by force, and even that limitation of your freedom will apply only to your body and not to your mind.

That is why love has been perverted into possession, because possession creates fear, and real freedom is only possible in the total absence of fear. And that is why we are taught to hate. Hatred is a chain that tethers you to the object of your hate, because as long as you hate your foes you will be granting them a pre-eminent place in your mind, and hence the power to control your whole life. Conversely, forgiveness is the key to freedom: you will only be truly free when you learn to love friends and enemies alike without any expectation, for unconditional love is the only razor capable of severing all your bonds.

That is why from our childhood on we are taught not to think. That is why when we grow up we are kept busy every second of our existence with a truckload of futile distractions. And that is why consumer societies cannot limit themselves to *offering* constant gratification of the existing desires of all their members, but they also need to *create* new desires all the time to maintain a permanent tension between the negative and positive poles of desire: craving and satisfaction.

Work, buy, sleep, and repeat! Work, but don't think! Click, but don't think! Watch, but don't think! Listen, but don't think! Buy, but don't think! Swallow, but don't think! Work more so that you can buy more, but don't think! Don't question anything, just obey! Dump you tired carcass on the armchair, sink into the sofa, open your eyes and ears to the mesmerizing oracle on the big flat screen, and gulp down everything like a sinkhole; as long as you *do not think*!

What? Is your mind tired? Good! Now you can go to bed, where our pointless monotonous lullaby will soon sweetly rock you into an empty sleep! Relax, for while you are snoring the night away we will take care of your world and get everything ready for tomorrow. We'll show you all the things you don't have, new excitement for your weary mind, and new ways to gratify your desires. Don't worry, though, because nothing fundamental will change; above all, there will be none of that new-fangled thinking! Intellectually, tomorrow will be just like today, just like yesterday, and just like every other day of your life.

So you're asking, "And then, what?" Well, you do know the answer, don't you? Oh yes, you do, and while we're on the subject, don't forget to work just a little bit harder, because the more you work, the more prestigious the final hole you will be able to afford! And if you are a very good boy, as a reward we'll put a very large stone on top of your mound for everyone to see, remember, and emulate!

Of course, it won't make a big difference to *you* anymore… but that's life!

FINAL THOUGHTS ON ATTACHMENT

I f you have experienced happiness before your possession of an object or a person, logically you should be able to experience happiness again if you lose that object or person!

Enjoy everything in life permanently in the present, without fear of losing it, without craving or attachment. Always remember that you only own your mind and body; all the rest has just been lent to you. Don't be misguided into considering material objects as possessions that "belong" to you, but see them instead as toys at your disposal in the infinite playground of creation. Play with them while you can, and have fun, but don't hog them. Stick to sharing and caring instead, because you'll have to leave everything behind when your time comes – and it will, though you never know when. Never forget that your house is just another hotel room, and you will soon have to check out, so always be ready to move on!

Drop the ballast of your attachments and glide smoothly through the eye of the needle.

Finally, love as much as you possibly can! Do the easy part first: Love your spouse, your family, your friends... But don't forget the hard stuff, and love your enemy too – it is more challenging, but ultimately much more rewarding. Love truly without expecting anything in return, and always enjoy the love you're given in the present without fear of the future, aware that it won't last forever.

As Epictetus wrote in his *Enchiridion,*

> *If you would have your children and your wife and your friends to live forever, you are silly; for you would have the things which are not in your power to be in your power, and the things which belong to others to be yours.*[9]

Possess, and you will remain a slave!
Love, and you shall be free!

II. THE "TOMORROW" MYTH

Never let the future ruin your present! Worrying about what might happen is like dining in an excellent restaurant and worrying about the price: You'll spoil your meal, and you'll still have to pay your bill anyway!

A LIFE FREE FROM
ANXIETY IS POSSIBLE

"There are things which are within our power, and there are things which are beyond our power." These lines, written two thousand years ago by the Greek stoic philosopher Epictetus[9], might seem to state the obvious, and yet they contain the key to overcoming all the worry and anxiety that haunts our mind.

As with all great ideas, this axiom is simple to understand, and yet few of us are willing to accept it and apply it fully to our own lives, probably because our ego is reluctant to admit that most things in life are beyond our power and that there is only one thing that we *can* control, and that is our mind.

Why is it of such critical importance to be aware at all times of the dividing line between what we can control and what we cannot, though? And why is this quote relevant in our quest to overcome worry and anxiety?

There are three major reasons. Firstly, because while, at least in theory, we have all the power to control our mind, there's little we can do about what lies out of it; indeed, *anything* outside our mind is beyond our power to control. Secondly, because, paradoxically, ninety-nine percent of our anxiety stems from things that are beyond our control. And thirdly, because, ironically, we squander our life trying to control the countless things that are beyond our power, while forgetting to focus on the very few things that we can control.

In fact, the best way to ruin your life with worry and anxiety is by trying to control events that are beyond your control, and most events in life belong to this category. The list includes the actions, feelings, reactions, and thoughts of other people; the decay of our bodies due to aging, accidents, and diseases; and, in general, everything that is not a product of our own mind.

We've been misguided into thinking that we can control things that we cannot, and, in spite of all the evidence against it, we refuse to admit that we are wrong. For instance, we have been led to believe that we can expect other people to respond to our actions with some sort of reciprocal and foreseeable reaction, but that is false. Although for a while there might appear to be some kind of correspondence between our acts and how other people react to them, the truth is that other people's reactions clearly belong to the realm of things that are beyond our power to control.

That is why worrying about what other people may or may not do, or about how they will react to your actions, is totally useless. We cannot control how other people interact with us; only how *we* interact with them and how *we* react to that interaction.

Besides, there is no universal law that stipulates that people must conduct themselves as you think they *should*, so the only power you have is to accept that they behave as they *do*, and adapt your reaction to their behavior. Whenever you expect other people to behave in a certain manner, you are bound to be disappointed, and remember that your disappointment only qualifies you, and never the person who has "disappointed" you. When they don't react as you thought they would or should, the fault, if any, is not with them, but with you. The mismatch between your expectations and what really happens does not mean that the other person's behavior is wrong, but that *your* assumptions about their behavior were wrong. In other words, when you say you are disappointed, you are merely admitting to your mistake, to your error of judgment, recognizing that *you* were wrong about the person you are disappointed with.

Exactly the same applies to events: We can only control those that are generated by our own actions: i.e., those that are a product of our mind. All the rest are beyond our control, and yet paradoxically, it is these events, the innumerable events beyond our power, that are the source of most of our worry and anxiety! How absurd, and yet, how true!

Many people are worried by the possibility of losing their jobs, suffering economic loss, or contracting a serious disease, and while preventive measures, such as a good performance at work, sound economic management, or a healthy lifestyle do help, in the end, there is not too much we can do to completely avoid these woes.

Let me make clear that this assertion is definitely not an apology of recklessness or apathy. On the contrary, the source of anxiety is the unwanted event, and not the prevention of it, so we can perfectly well lead a purposeful life trying to avoid these negative events without feeling the need to worry about them! Furthermore, as we shall see below, anxiety is always about the future, while prevention takes place in the present; and we never worry about the present, only about the future.

There is also another compelling reason we have to learn to focus on what we can control, and not on what we cannot. Trying to control anything that is beyond our power is a waste of our limited time and energy, which will thus not be available to allow us to pay full attention to the present. That is why people who worry too much are inefficient, and that is why people who are less afraid of what may happen in the future are so effective. While the former show a deep aversion to risk because they are paralyzed by the thought of all the things that could possibly go wrong, the latter are always willing to take risks because they know that they cannot control the future anyway, and so they live fully immersed in the present, trust their gut feelings, and act on them. And if most successful people have gone through countless failures, losses and setbacks it is precisely because they have been willing to give chance a chance! If you never try, you will never fail, but you will never advance either. As always, it's your choice.

The last argument against worrying is that whereas you have little control over a lot of what happens to you, you *always* have the power to decide how you react. And this power is all you need to be happy at all times. It is independent of any external factor; it is an inbuilt mechanism in your mind that is, and will always be, available to you.

Finally, as Seneca put it: "There are more things, Lucilius, likely to frighten us than there are to crush us; we suffer more often in imagination than in reality."[10] How often have you spent time worrying about something which could happen in the future and then it never did? And even in those few instances when it did happen, how often did you realize with relief that it wasn't that bad as you feared it would be? Whatever happens, worrying about it doesn't help. On the contrary, worrying about future events just fills your present with fear. And remember: If you are able to face adversity in the present, you will also be able to face it in what we like to call "the future," which is in reality no more than your next present.

> *Be not disturbed about the future, for if ever you come to it, you will have the same reason for your guide which preserves you at present.*
>
> Marcus Aurelius[11]

FUTURE TENSE, OR TENSE FUTURE?

> *Therefore, do not worry about tomorrow, for tomorrow will worry about itself. Each day has enough trouble of its own.*
>
> Matthew 6:34[4]

Most of the anxiety that troubles our present is caused by *the fear of events that may happen in the future*. Even though most of these *possible* future tragedies never actually happen, they haunt our imagination and ruin our present life.

Anxiety is thus an irrational fear caused by something that only exists in our imagination, but the suffering it causes is real. We imagine loss, disease, poverty, and death in the future, but we suffer in the present, and we live in constant fear of the products of our own mind. When disease, poverty or death happen (i.e., they become a reality in the present), then we can no longer talk about anxiety, but only of fear, suffering, pain...

We are constantly creating this fictitious "future" to escape from the only reality we have, the present, and then we believe that our creation is real: so real that we do not hesitate to sacrifice our present happiness for it.

If you worry all the time, your present is always characterized by worry. And since your life is just a succession of present moments, you live your entire life as a victim of your own anxiety.

He who fears he shall suffer, already suffers what he fears.

Michel de Montaigne[6]

On the other hand, when you experience the bliss of one single present without any worry or anxiety, you understand the meaning of untarnished happiness. Einstein once said that a happy man is too satisfied with the present to dwell too much on the future. Try it, experience the bliss of a mind free from worry, and you'll want more and more of it.

To sum up, we are constantly creating in our mind unreal images of ourselves that we know are not happening in the now, so we have to choose another "time" to place them in, and, according to our (mis-)conception of time, we can only choose between the "past" and the "future". Since we know the events we are imagining never actually happened, we cannot place them in the past, so the most commonly accepted option is to take for real a fantasy called "the future" onto which we can project our own image, like an avatar, experiencing whatever events we decide to conjure up in our mind.

> For the difference is not great between fearing a danger, and feeling it; except that the evil one feels has some bounds, whereas one's apprehensions have none. For we can suffer no more than what actually has happened but we fear all that possibly could happen.
>
> Pliny the Younger[12]

Now, here is my proposal for your consideration: Since we constantly create our future in our mind in the present, and then we decide our fate in that future which only exists in our imagination, why not only imagine a bright future in which *exclusively* good things happen to you? If you learn to change your mindset into a positive one, you will soon realize that it takes exactly the same effort to imagine yourself enjoying good health, happiness, and success as it does to imagine a future full of adversity.

In other words, why imagine misery when you can imagine bliss?

SOME STATISTICS

For the mass media, it seems that the only news is "bad news." It usually presents a distorted view of the world, selectively showing only the morbid side of reality, without giving the whole context, which would put most of the catastrophic events in their proper perspective.

If there's an airplane crash, the news channels will concentrate on the number of casualties but they will all omit to inform the audience that this accident is only an exception to the rule, flying being by far the safest mode of transportation. And since most people only get to see the dark side, they naturally extrapolate the partial and selective information they get from the media, generalize it, and reach conclusions that are totally false. The saddest of all is that their flawed assumptions make them live in a permanent state of anxiety.

On average, while many people are anxious about flying in an airplane, only a few are afraid of traveling by car, and even fewer of walking. Why? Because a car accident or a dead pedestrian is not catastrophic enough to be news anymore. As a result, an airplane crash that kills two hundred people will immediately become breaking news worldwide, and all the media will devote special coverage to a terrorist attack that causes the same number of casualties, but no media will report that more than three thousand people die *every single day* in road accidents around the world. And even less probable is that the 740 pedestrians killed *every day* in traffic accidents will make the headlines.

Let me give you some statistical data that may surprise you if you have been watching the news too much. In the ten years between 2006 and 2016, 584 people on average died per year due to air traffic accidents, which means an average of 1.6 deaths per day.

At the same time, nearly 1.3 million(!) people die in road accidents each year, with an additional 20–50 million injured or disabled, which gives an average of approximately 3,200 dead and 96,000 injured every single day of the year!

In other words, on average, the same number

of people die every four hours in road accidents as in a whole year in air traffic accidents!

In addition, according to the WHO, more than 270,000 pedestrians lose their lives on the world's roads each year (740 per day), which means that on any given day more pedestrians will be killed in road accidents than in a whole year in air traffic accidents. But again, a dead pedestrian does not make the headlines!

On the same theme, between 2011 and 2016 natural disasters caused a yearly average of 14,193 deaths, and during the same period, 19,720 people died each year on average in terrorist attacks. Now compare these two figures with the massive 17.7 *million* people who died from cardiovascular diseases in 2015 alone – an average of 48,493 deaths per day – which means that more people die every day from cardiovascular disease than all the casualties from natural disasters and terrorist attacks together in one entire year!

Despite this, for many people the level of anxiety caused by the possibility of becoming victims of a terrorist attack or a natural disaster is higher than the anxiety induced by the possibility of suffering from cardiovascular disease; and people who panic every time they have to fly take to their cars every day with no sign of worry or anxiety.

Although the statistical examples above may

not be 100% comparable, they do give an accurate idea of the real risk that each of these "dangers" poses. The point is that not only are people anxious about things that are beyond their control, but on top of that they are anxious about the very events that are least likely to beset them.

FINAL THOUGHTS ON THE FUTURE

D eath is always around us. But since we fear her company, we try by all means to distance ourselves from her, in particular by creating an imaginary buffer between us and our death. That buffer is what we call "the future."

The future exists only in our imagination, and in that illusory interlude between our present and our death we imagine all sorts of calamities, and then we worry about them – and, since we have a tendency to fill empty spaces, the longer the interlude, the more reasons to worry we create in it. However, the opposite is also true: The shorter the interlude, the fewer calamities we can fit inside it – and to take it to its logical conclusion, if there is no interlude at all, we simply stop worrying.

Why is this so fundamental? Because in the presence of death, everything loses its importance, all our worries vanish, and we can't help but admit that the world will keep on turning without us.

Death relativizes the value of everything, so that the only absolute value left is that of *life*; and not of any kind of life, but of life in the present – the only life there is.

Immortality is a bore: life has value precisely because it is finite.

I myself had to face death in my early twenties in order to wake up from my anorexic daymare and start living. And ever since that day, the awareness of death is what keeps me alive. But don't wait until you see *your* death before you start to live: it might be too late!

As long as we have a mind and we are alive, we have all we need to be happy in the here and now, because happiness exists only in the mind, and the expression of our mind takes place while we are alive, in the present. And that is why we should not be concerned about anything that could happen in that fantasy called "the future" – let alone about anything that could come after our death.

By suggesting the above, I am neither accepting nor denying that we might have an independent eternal soul or spirit (call it what you will) which will survive our body, and migrate to a Heaven, a Hell, a Nirvana, a Jannah, a Shamayim, or any other *place* after our physical death. What I am saying is that either way it is simply irrelevant to our objective, namely, that of finding practical ways to make the present moment, which is really all we have, better

If you believe that there is a life after death, that's great, I fully respect it – after all, I have no reason to believe that there is no life after death. However, the point I'm making is this: Do not allow your belief in a life after death to interfere with your happiness in this definitely real life!

Paraphrasing Casanova's words, "Since the only way to know with certainty that there is a life after death is by dying, I'll be forgiven for not being in a hurry to acquire such knowledge, considering the high price I would have to pay for it."

And, even if we are convinced of the existence of life after death, why waste the certainty of the bliss we could be enjoying today in exchange for the promise of a vague and uncertain happiness?

Live the present the best you can, as death will arrive anyway; and if there is another life after this one, don't hurry: you will eventually get there to enjoy it.

Every time you sacrifice your present happiness on the altar of an imaginary future you become your worst enemy, and on your deathbed, your conscience will judge you and declare you guilty of the worst crime you could commit against yourself: not having lived your life to the fullest. Always weigh your actions on the balance of your self-actualization, and if you find them wanting, change. Don't wait until tomorrow, next week, or next month. Stop fooling yourself with the false hope that there'll be a better time to change, because there will not.

Today's the day. Seize it!

AFTERWORD

You may well live somebody else's life, but you will always die your own death, so why not be yourself, live as you will, and have fun while you can?

JACK'S STORY

During one of my travels in Canada, I met a very special person called Jack, the owner of a small campground somewhere on the country's rugged Pacific coast. He was a tall, thin and shaggy man in his late fifties, casually dressed in torn shorts and a faded T-shirt. There was nothing pretentious about him, and yet the power of his presence struck me the very first time I saw him. He had an aura of dignity, peace, enlightenment, and bliss such as I have never found in any of the kings, presidents, and celebrities I have had the chance to work for in my professional life.

Jack was the silent type, so after a crisp greeting upon arriving at the campground, and a few essential instructions while checking in, he just took me to my campsite without a word and immediately left.

I put up my tent, ate something, read for an hour, rigged up my fishing tackle, and headed to the shore, looking for a good place to try to hook some salmon. I walked along the high, rocky coastline, trying to find an accessible cove, until I finally saw a promising place to cast my line, but as I got closer I saw in the dim light of the sunset the tip of a rod moving among the boulders. Somebody had already chosen that spot. I was just about to turn around to avoid disturbing this other fisherman when I realized he was silently waving at me, unmistakably inviting me to join him.

I knew I could do with some advice, as I was totally unfamiliar with that part of the coast, so I did not hesitate for a second to go down to where he was. Maybe he could tell me where to fish, which lures to use, and what was the best tide to fish on.

I scrambled my way down to him full of anticipation and, to my surprise, as I got close enough I realized that the person who was so effortlessly waltzing among the boulders was none other than Jack, the owner of the campground.

He greeted me with just a smile, and, without uttering any sound, he pointed to the place where his line disappeared in the iridescent glare of the last rays of sunshine reflected on the broken mirror of the ocean. He was slowly reeling in his lure, making it dance under the surface through a perfect performance of sharp pulls of the tip of his rod, imbuing it with the miracle of life by transmitting his own animation to the inert piece of metal swimming underwater. The sight of him was awesome! He was no longer just a fisherman on the shore, but a fisher-mutant. The tackle was part of his body, the rod was the natural extension of his arm, the line the continuation of his hand, the lure the expression of his will; and he was as one with the rocks, the kelp, the sun, and the ocean.

I dared not move. I felt like a child in the presence of a divine power, witnessing a supernatural event; an unscheduled guest whose presence in that world would be tolerated only so long as I did not do anything to break the magic of the moment.

All of a sudden something pulled hard on the slightly slack line until it became so tight that it began to whistle in the breeze, like the hum of a gigantic single-stringed violin played by the invisible hand of the wind.

The silent moment lasted for an endless second while Jack stared into my eyes, motionless like a statue, then he looked away to the ocean while jerking his rod sharply to set the hook, and instantly everything exploded in the crimson twilight as a massive salmon leapt out of the water.

Jack fought the salmon carefully but steadily all the way to the shore, where I helped him pull it out of the water. It was a huge chinook easily over thirty pounds, a rare catch, probably even for Jack – at least that is what I thought. I felt an urge to share my excitement with him, but as I opened my mouth he raised his finger, urging me to stay quiet; and how right he was, for there was nothing to be said.

It was getting late, so we walked back together in silence to the campground, where Jack led me to the fish-cleaning station located in a small detached wooden hut. He quickly gutted and filleted the salmon with the dexterity of an experienced sushi cook, so effortlessly that he made the delicate task look easy as pie.

When he was done, Jack washed off the blood and scales from the cutting desk with the cracked grey hose secured to the faucet with duct tape, wiped his hands with a dirty towel, and put the clean fillets inside a plastic bag. Then he opened the large off-white chest freezer in the corner, put the bag inside, and ushered me out of the hut.

I followed him along the narrow track leading to his house, which was a small log cabin with a large unpaved porch on its western side.

"The sunsets around here are beautiful," he muttered finally as he sat down on an old rocking chair in the porch, without turning around towards me. "I still enjoy them after so many years."

I waited to be offered a seat, but he remained silent, motionlessly staring into the distance as if he was trying to catch the last warming rays of the setting sun.

"May I?" I asked politely, pointing to the other chair, which, together with a sturdy stool, was the only furniture in the porch.

He finally looked at me and nodded, but almost instantly he turned his gaze again towards the orange western horizon, and just as if he could read my thoughts, he whispered, still staring into the distance:

"I don't talk much in general, but while I'm fishing I don't talk *at all*. Hope you don't take it personally."

"Of course not," I said apologetically, "It's just that I wanted to tell you that..."

"... that you were impressed by that last catch?" he interrupted.

"Yes," I admitted, "I've never seen anything like that before."

"Like what?" He probed. "Like that thirty-pounder king?"

"No, that's not what I meant. I've been fishing myself for the last thirty-five years, and I've sort of gotten used to seeing big fish..." I paused, looked at him, and then I continued. "It's the way it happened: You seemed to be in a kind of trance, as if you were not of this world, but part of the ocean... you were, how should I say...?"

"Absorbed?"

"Yes, that's exactly what I mean," I confirmed to him.

"Presence," Jack whispered, and, almost immediately, he stared into my eyes again, and repeated emphatically, "*Presence.*"

Then he stared again towards the sunset, and just when I thought I had lost him again, he continued:

"A while ago – on the shore I mean – I was there," he added softly in his deep voice, "there, and nowhere else. I could *feel* that king chasing the lure long before it hit it. And I knew exactly when he would bite it... but I'm no wizard, at least not of the kind you think. When you are truly present in the here and now magic happens, but it's not a supernatural kind of magic. It's human magic, and it's there for the taking, available to everyone, except most people are blind. We see when we are born, and we see while we are children, but as we grow up our eyes are gradually misted over with a haze of lies: lies about wealth, power, fame, needs, time, problems... and we believe them, and we live blinded by our own inner darkness, so we fail to see that there are no problems, no worries, no fear in this wonderful world, but only in our mind. And the worst thing is that most people die blind, deprived forever of a life that they never truly lived," Jack said impassionedly, raising his voice for the first time in the whole day. "Blind... they're all stone blind!"

Suddenly, Jack paused, looked down, and sighed, "...and so was I."

I was puzzled by these words. Jack looked like the happiest man on Earth, so I could not help but interrupt him:

"But you look at peace with yourself and with the world too. And you look totally happy."

"I am," he reassured me, still looking down, and remained silent for a short while as if he was trying to recollect something. "I am... now, but it hasn't always been like that. The harsh truth is that I wasted the best years of my life before I came to realize that I had totally misunderstood the meaning of life. But that's a long story... a personal story."

"Would you mind sharing it with me?" I asked with a keen sense of curiosity.

He stared at me again and said slowly,

"All right, then."

"I haven't told this story to anyone in a long time, and I have no idea why I'm telling it to you; in fact, I don't remember telling *anything* particular to *anyone* in years, but you look truly interested and I feel like talking tonight, so here it is...

"Before I started to work in my mid-twenties I had no idea of what worry and anxiety meant. Until then I'd lived a carefree life, doing the things that I loved to do – you know, mostly fishing and reading books. As a child I enjoyed going to school, and later, I also had fun while studying my university degree. I had a nonchalant attitude towards everything in life.

"Then something happened. I began to worry. First, I started to worry about my job, which I believed to be a completely normal thing because that's what everybody else around me was doing. Then I got married, and started to worry about my relationship, as everybody else did. Then my wife and I had children, and I began to worry for them, just as everybody else did... and so on, until my entire life was full of worry and anxiety.

At the same time, looking back on those days I can't find any real justification for my anxiety. I was in good health, had a well-remunerated job in a big business, everyone liked me, my family loved me... I had nothing to worry about, and yet my whole life was miserable. My life was permanently haunted by anxiety, and the more I worried, the more reasons I had to worry. This is one of the biggest ironies of life! I once read this joke somewhere: 'Who says worrying is useless? It's certainly useful – every time I worry about something it never happens'... how true, Sonny, how true!"

He paused, pulled up the sleeve of his shirt, and showed me his wristwatch.

"Look! See the second hand of my watch? It

won't stop. The seconds flow away relentlessly, one after the other, and that's what we call life; and that's all we got; and it sort of goes away without you noticing it because you're inside of it, and then one night you go to bed and the next morning you don't wake up. That's life, and that's exactly what I wasted.

"Days, weeks, and months went by, and I was unable to see the beauty around me through the thick veil of anxiety that gnawed away what little happiness and peace of mind I still had, until there was no more left. My children left home, some years later my wife left too, each fresh summer greeted a new fall, and every fall welcomed a new winter, but I was still too blind to notice this beautiful life. In the meantime, though, the sands of time continued to fall relentlessly, and the seasons slowly took away my youth with them, until one morning a wrinkled, gray-haired old man looked at me from inside the mirror.

"I grew prematurely old, and in my late forties I began to feel a particular kind of sickness, like a strong nausea; first sporadically, but as time went by it became almost permanent. For a while, I thought this feeling was just an inevitable part of aging, but after some months I made up my mind and went to see a doctor.

"Well, I was diagnosed with cancer, and the doctor told me sensitively that, unless I underwent major treatment immediately, in six months I'd most likely be departed. I remember receiving the bad news coldly, almost with indifference, to the doctor's surprise. Of course, I never told him that I couldn't see any point in prolonging a life such as the one I was living. I just thanked him and walked out of the hospital to the parking lot. It was a cold Vancouver morning; the strong on-shore breeze submerged the city in a dense salty mist that suddenly took me back to the days when, right after moving to Vancouver, I used to go fishing along the Fraser River every single day after the job – happy days that were long gone.

"I got into my car and headed mechanically towards the modern glass-tiled office-building where I worked, but something happened while I was waiting for the first traffic light. I felt dizzy again, but now in a most peculiar way, as if the time had stopped. I fainted – or at least I believe I did – and then, suddenly, I had a vision that made me shudder: Whirling inside a dark mist I saw the waxy image of my own corpse. My own inert body was right there before me, lying on a white hospital couch, with my lifeless hands clasped over my belly. I watched it for what seemed an eternity to me, until a sudden strident noise brought me back to the present. The light had turned green, probably quite a while ago, and the drivers behind me were honking like madmen. I started the car and drove on till the next intersection, and there I knew I had to make a decision right there and then that I had been postponing for years: I had to choose between continuing to live like a robot the scarce time I had left, and living the life I had always wanted to live.

"I decided on the spot that I had to get out of the rat race, that I didn't want to die in the office. I decided to quit everything, and the first necessary step was to resign from my job, a job that I despised, but had been afraid to leave… until now. For a few seconds, I entertained the foolish idea of carrying on working for a couple of weeks, just until… but that was what I had been saying for the last twenty years: "just until tomorrow." But now "tomorrow" just meant "death," and I knew that this time it had to be drastic; it had to be all or nothing.

"I made the only sensible decision I could have made in those circumstances, and chose to immediately start living my life in my own way. So I made a U-turn and headed home. On the way back, for a while I still visualized my desk in the office, full of important unfinished work, and I began to worry about the colleagues I was letting down. I felt I was betraying them, to the point that I almost drove back to the office to at least finish the most urgent matters, but I quickly dismissed the thought. I was inescapably sliding down the one-way street of life, headlong towards death, and in a few months the world would have to do without me anyway, so they'd better start getting used to it; and the sooner the better.

"I parked my car in my front yard, and after the usual five-minute key search I finally opened the entrance door and went into the kitchen. I looked around while I prepared some coffee, and all I could see were dust-covered useless objects that I had gathered over a lifetime, and that now meant nothing to me. The whole space was filled with "stuff," and yet, it was so devoid of warmth and happiness that compared to it a graveyard was an amusement park. I could not even remember where most of those objects came from. How did they get there? Who were they from? Why did I get them?

"Not only had I not seen or touched them for years, but, for some unknown reason, I had been actively avoiding contact with them, even seeing them, to the point that my whole house had long ago become an irksome dodgem circuit among dusty obstacles that I had to negotiate between the front door, the kitchen, and my bed.

"To tell you the truth, from the day my children and my wife left me, my house ceased to be my home, so I was kind of used to the lonesome and messy place. But that day it looked even worse. I felt as a dying pharaoh inside a gloomy pyramid full of rotten food and meaningless rubbish to feed and entertain my putrefying corpse for all eternity.

"The only sign of life in the whole house was a lonesome red rock crab that I kept in an oversized aquarium. I'd had it for quite a while – I even gave it a name! I called it J.B. because, on account of its flaming color, it reminded me of Johnny Blaze, the Ghost Rider... my favorite comic hero in my twenties. I guess it kept me good company... you know. J.B. was the kind of guy who'd always listen to you without butting in! Now I suddenly felt sorry for him, watching how after all this time he was still hopelessly searching for a crack in the aquarium's walls to reach the ocean he was taken from, displaying his flaming anger in the glass jail in which he was serving a cruel and unjust life sentence.

"I stared at him and thought that maybe someone was looking at us too from above, also feeling sorry for our fate, while we were working and living like ants in our cold glass buildings. The difference is that whereas wild animals never truly give up, we humans don't even try to break free anymore. We tend to surrender our freedom without a fight. Maybe we're already like those poor zoo-born beasts, unable to survive in the wilderness if released. Generations of self-imposed slavery have eroded our natural wild instincts.

"I wrote a short letter of resignation while I

drank my coffee, and, boy, how light I felt when I was done! Then I went down to the basement to dig out my fishing gear from underneath a huge heap of useless trash.

"I finally managed to rescue a couple of rods and reels in working condition, together with a box of faded lures and my waders, and dumped everything in the trunk. Then I went back into the house, picked up a large bucket, immersed it in the aquarium, put J.B. inside it, secured it on the passenger's seat, and drove down to a spot where I used to fish with my father when I was a child.

"As soon as I was on the shore I felt better. The cold wet wind woke me up as I filled my lungs with the smell of the ocean, and the contrast between the dark cluttered prison of my house and the bright clean freedom of the beach made me forget all my troubles, at least for a while.

"The first thing I did was to bid farewell to Mister Johnny Blaze, who quickly disappeared among the boulders. Then I opened the dirty lure box and randomly picked a yellow spoon, tied it to the line, and cast it as far as I could. I reeled it in slowly, paying attention to every inch of line on the spool, visualizing the spoon as I made it swirl on its way towards the shore… and the magic feeling started to come back. My racing thoughts slowed down with every turn of the handle, and all I knew was that I felt something I hadn't felt for years: profound peace of mind and absolute happiness.

"It was the first time in a long time I was having fun, and that I didn't feel the choking oppression of anxiety on my chest. How could I worry about anything when I'd soon be dead? I visualized myself in all the situations that I'd feared so much, like being fired from my job and deprived of my possessions, and losing everything I had... and now I simply didn't give a damn anymore because I *knew* I would soon lose everything anyway! At last, nothing else mattered but the present.

"I fished for hours, I fished until it was so dark that I could no longer see anything around me, and only then did I realize that, apart from a coffee, I hadn't eaten or drunk anything the whole day – and yet I was neither hungry nor thirsty. Above all, I realized with awe that I didn't know for how many hours in a row I had totally forgotten about my job, my disease, and my emotional emptiness. In a very long time, this was the first day that I had been alive, just that: *alive*.

"Right then and there, I made up my mind to live the time left to me as fully as I could, and it was only then that I truly discovered the meaning of the present, and I understood that the future is just an invention of our minds confirmed by education, which converts this aberration of time into a dogma, a collective belief. I decided to be happy, period, and I was positive I could do it, for now I had nothing to lose. I could easily die any day, any hour, any minute.

"It's ironic to think that after almost a half-century treading this Earth I only realized that I was alive when I saw my death coming. After so many years as a walking dead man, life came to me from where I least expected it, for only in the ashes of demise did I find the force that could lit the fire of my existence with such an uncontainable spark.

"The awareness that I could finally be happy changed me radically. Just a few hours earlier in the hospital I didn't care about dying, but now I wanted desperately to survive, and have more of this long-forgotten bliss called "life." I decided I would do anything to overcome the disease and live. I was eventually operated on and received heavy medication, then I had a second operation... I'll spare you the gory details.

"Strangely enough, those were hard times for my body, but not for my mind. People around me thought I must be miserable, but in reality, I was happier than ever before. I was a wreck physically, but mentally I'd become a giant. I was finally free from all the heavy ballast of worry and anxiety I'd been pointlessly carrying, like Sisyphus' boulder, for almost all my adult life.

"After a difficult year, and against all expectations, the doctors said I was healed, or at least as healed as I could ever be. The illness was gone, but it had taken a heavy toll on my body: I was bald, grey and emaciated. However, underneath all those traumatic visible and invisible scars, the disease had left me a hidden jewel, a precious gift: It had freed me from all worry and anxiety for good. After all the pain, not only my body but also my mind was healed. Physically, I recovered very fast, probably because now I had a reason to live, and I wanted to enjoy my new life, to be fully self-sufficient, to go fishing again. Mentally, it was like waking up to a new morning after a nightmare only to find myself stronger than I had been before the disease. I never ever worried again. Such is the power of the mind.

"Why did I not change before, while I still had a whole healthy life before me? Why did I need to feel the cold blade of the somber scythe on my neck? Why did I need to see the dark shadow of the Grim Reaper standing over me?

"I've been looking for a satisfactory answer to these questions ever since that day, but I've still not found it. And it's probably not that easy to understand why we toil and suffer from worry instead of living this wonderful life in the present, because if it was easy, everybody would be living a happy life.

"Since I had quit my job, during my treatment, I had plenty of time to waste, so I wandered around aimlessly, trying to spot happy people down in the city. I looked for them out in the streets, in the shopping malls, in the parks... I searched for them everywhere, and all I could see when I looked around me were wrinkled foreheads, dull eyes, and alienated people who seemed to be anywhere except in the present moment.

"That's why I left behind what people like to call "civilization" once the healing was complete. There was nothing for me there anymore: no family, no friends, and no job... only a house that had not been my home for a long, long time, and which was more of a burden than anything else. I decided to move to any place remote enough that I didn't have to meet people. A place where I could fish every day till I die, alone like a stray dog, but in peace at last. I sold my house and looked at a map to see where I could go, and luckily, I didn't have to go too far away, because this part of the country is full of such remote places. I traveled around the province for a while, mainly along the coast, until I found this cove. It has nothing special, I know, but I just fell in love with it as soon as I saw it, and I still do love it. Anyway, it's good enough for me, and that's the only thing that matters.

"With the money I got from the sale of the house I bought this property, which was then just a plot of vacant land. I built a log cabin and fished around for a couple of years. Then, as my money was starting to run short, I realized I had to do something for a living, so I opened this campground – not really expecting much to come of it, because I couldn't imagine why people would come here at all. Anyway, I didn't care about anything anymore – I just felt good here, and that was enough.

"I almost forgot something important, though! Do you remember the way I said my house was full of objects? Well, I gave away everything I could, and dumped all the rest in the landfill... and d'you know? Not only did I feel much lighter, but for some reason also much younger! In fact, the only objects that I keep from the past are some pictures of my family, and my fishing gear... Oh, yes! and that vintage board on the wall", said Jack as he pointed to a faded, square tin board fixed to the wall, halfway between the door and the only window that looked onto the porch.

"Can you read it?" he asked hesitantly.

I could, and I read it aloud. It said, "Life is short! Break the rules, forgive quickly, kiss slowly, love truly, laugh uncontrollably and never regret anything that made you smile. Mark Twain."

"Good!" he replied loudly, but then he paused,

and continued in a low, melancholic voice:

"I used to have that board hanging somewhere in my kitchen, but I never really took it seriously... but now I do! And if more people around the world did too, our life would be altogether different, so much better. But nobody really does. People prefer to waste their lives lost in the mess of their petty problems, trying to be better than everybody else, and trampling other people underfoot in their fight for power and glory. That's why I quit society.

"You know, Sonny? You can call me a coward, but I admit that when I came here, I was also escaping from my past, and kind of shunning civilization. I felt imprisoned there and wanted to get out of that pack for good. And so I did!

"However, as time went by something changed inside of me. I grew kinder, or I should rather say that happiness made me a kinder person in comparison to the one I was before I had the disease and left everything behind. For a long time, I didn't feel any urge to share my experience with anyone... but I do now, probably in an attempt to wake people up… and that's the only reason I'm boring you now with my story."

"You're not boring me, Jack; on the contrary, I totally lost the notion of time while I was listening to you," I said, and it was true. "Please, go on, if you will."

"Good. I'm almost done. I realized quite late that I'd spent all my life in Paradise without knowing it, but not too late though, and I've definitely made amends ever since. Hard as it was to admit it, I finally came to accept that I'd wasted most of my life and that there's nothing in the world I could do to get back even a second of all the time I lost – I have to live with that... but I'm happy that I changed, late as it was. I squandered some twenty-five years of my existence. Twenty-five years wasting a healthy body from dawn to dusk in a fifty-five-square-foot cubicle with no natural light, wasting precisely what should have been the best years of my life, until looming death opened my eyes to see this marvelous reality in which I had always been living – and now I want to share this vision with as many people as I possibly can... as I'm sharing it with you now. I'm almost 65 now, and for the last fifteen years, my life has been full of happiness; so full that now I feel compelled to give this bliss back to the world, to make it a better place. I wish I could reach out to the young around the world and tell them to stop worrying, to learn to face their death every day, to be free, and to be themselves no matter what price they have to pay for it. Happiness is an infinite resource, and it's all around us... and it's all around you too, Sonny – you just have to open your eyes and enjoy it, just as I've been enjoying every hour, every minute, and every second of my life ever since I rediscovered happiness."

"What's the secret?" I asked, but then quickly added, "I mean, I understand that worrying about anything that could happen to us is totally useless, that anxiety is an irrational fear that has no real cause, and I can see how it ruined the best years of your life, but in practice how can I totally eradicate all worry and anxiety from my life?"

He looked at me intensely, and, after a short silence, he uttered this proclamation:

"Just stop trying to control things that are beyond your power – and accept that most things are... and, above all, stop trying to live in the future! Learn to live in the present, and all worry and anxiety will naturally disappear from your life. And it makes sense too, for not only is it impossible to live in the future, but, worse still, it will deprive you of the only thing that you really have, which is the present. And don't take it lightly, Sonny, because "present" and "life" are synonymous, so when you squander your present, you're squandering your life. Just stay in the "now," and since the now can only happen in the "here," you will automatically be present in time and space, which is the only reality there is. All the rest is just a bunch of wretched lies that have kept you asleep for years; so wake up right now, and get a life!"

Then he said no more. We remained motionless for a while, silently breathing the cool evening air, full of turpentine and sea salt, until he stood up and walked slowly towards his cabin. He was already holding the knob when he paused, turned back, and said from beneath his doorway:

"Just remember this: Wake up... before it's too late!"

He then disappeared into his cabin, and I was left to myself. I remained there for what must have been quite a long while because by the time I started towards my tent I was shivering with cold.

I stayed in Jack's campground for almost a whole week, but we did not talk again, apart from a short casual greeting when we stumbled upon each other. He had told me everything he wanted, and he knew well that any further conversation was pointless. On the day of my departure, while packing my tent, I thought about how I could let him know how profoundly his story had changed me, so I decided to go to his cabin with some lame excuse and tell him. When I approached his hut I saw him sitting in the porch, and he must have heard me because he turned to look at me, so I began walking faster. However, as I got closer and our eyes met I realized there was nothing to say. Somehow, he *knew* everything, and it was clear that he was not expecting anything from me, so I just went up to him and shook his hand, but when I was about to withdraw my hand from his he held on to it, and with his other hand pulled out a piece of paper from his pocket and handed it to me.

"You'll read it later, Sonny," he whispered. "Now it's time for you to leave. Farewell!"

I took the piece of paper, put it in my pocket, and simply said, "Thank you, Jack!"

Then I left.

No sooner had I left the camp than I pulled up at the side of the road to read Jack's note. It was a quote:

> *Let hopes and sorrows, fears and angers be,*
> *And think each day that dawns the last you'll see;*
> *For so the hour that greets you unforeseen*
> *Will bring with it enjoyment twice as keen.*

Horace[13]

I never saw Jack again, but the memory of that day has remained so vivid in my mind that for all these years I have felt Jack's presence around me, like a protective spirit, constantly whispering words of redemption into my ear, urging me to wake up from my dream and start to live. I hope, dear reader, that he will keep you company too, and help you change your life.

HAPPINESS IS THE ROAD

D ear reader, this is the point where we part ways, for we have reached the end of our journey together. I thank you for your company and bid you farewell on your passage across the ocean of life. May favorable winds of change always fill your sails and lead you to new horizons of freedom and bliss – but never forget to enjoy the trip!

Every morning, when you wake up, think that this day may well be your last!

Admire this beautiful world, share your joy, and give love – with no limits!

Do what you love! And do it now! Future happiness is just a delusion. Saying that you don't have time today to do what you really love simply means that you don't have time to live – and you live but once.

Is there anything beyond? Does it matter at all? The road is more important than the place you're heading to, for tomorrow never comes, and there is no road to happiness. Happiness *is* the road, and that road is your life.

Your past is gone for good, and your future has never been more than a vague projection of your current dreams onto a tomorrow that will never come. But somewhere in between there exists a magic moment called the present – and that is the only thing you've really got, and it's the only thing you really need. It's a miracle... a miracle called life.

Jump confidently into the blissful ocean of the eternal present, swim in the seas of delight, and drench your heart with joy!

May we shatter the obscure chains of fear,
and break free at last,
Of the excruciating uncertainty of the future;
Of the unbearable burden of the past.
Dust within, dust without,
We are but a speck of dust,
Bound to be scattered by the wind,
Bound to sink and disappear
In the endless sands of time.
And yet alive we are
In the eternity of the now:
Wanton happiness,
Forever boundless,
In this wonderful Paradise.

***

Get a life and enjoy it!
Villa Marie, Barbados, January 7, 2019

REFERENCES

1 *The Teaching of Buddha.* © 1966 by Bukkyo Dendo Kyokai, Tokyo, Japan.

2 CASANOVA, GIACOMO GIROLAMO. *Mémoires de J. Casanova de Seingalt, écrits par lui-même.* Garnier Frères, Paris, 1880. Translated by Alberto Vezendi from the original French.

3 HELLIWELL, J., LAYARD, R., & SACHS, J. *World Happiness Report 2017.* Sustainable Development Solutions Network, New York, 2017.

4 *The Holy Bible.* New International Version®, NIV® ©1973, 1978, 1984, 2011 by Biblica, Inc.® Used by permission. All rights reserved worldwide.

5 THOREAU, HENRY DAVID. *Walden; or, Life in the Woods.* Ticknor & Fields, Boston, 1854.

6 MONTAIGNE, MICHEL EYQUEM DE. *Essays of Michel de Montaigne.* Translated by Charles Cotton. Edited by William Carew Hazlitt. A. L. Burt, New York, 1877.

7 ORWELL, GEORGE. *Nineteen-Eighty-Four.* Secker & Warburg, London, 1949.

[8] MILL, JOHN STUART. *On Liberty*. Longmans, Green & Co., London, 1867.

[9] EPICTETUS. *The Enchiridion*. Translated by George Long. George Bell and Sons, London, 1890.

[10] SENECA THE YOUNGER (LUCIUS ANNAEUS SENECA). "Epistle XIII: On groundless fears." *Moral Letters to Lucilius*. Translated by Richard Mott Gummere. Loeb Classical Library, William Heinemann, London, 1925.

[11] AURELIUS, MARCUS. *The Meditations of Marcus Aurelius*. Book VII, 8. Translated by Jeremy Collier. Revised by Alice Zimmern. Walter Scott, London, 1887.

[12] PLINY THE YOUNGER (GAIUS PLINIUS CAECILIUS SECUNDUS). *The Letters of Pliny The Younger*. Translated by William Melmoth, revised by Bosanquest. Hinds, Noble & Eldredge, New York, 1900.

[13] HORACE (QUINTUS HORATIUS FLACCUS). *The Satires, Epistles, and Art of Poetry of Horace*. Translated into English verse by John Conington. George Bell & Sons, London, 1874.

About the author

Of Hungarian origin, Alberto Vezendi arrived in Spain in 1979 at the age of six. A citizen of the world, he spent his summers travelling around Europe, mostly on his own, until he finally soared away from the nest in 1998. He left Spain after finishing his university studies with a master's degree and settled in Paris. There he started a career as a conference interpreter that would take him all around the world. For the next fifteen years his life was divided between four countries until in 2013 he landed on the serene shores of Lake Geneva, where he still lives today.

A NOTE FROM THE AUTHOR

Thank you for reading this book! I hope you enjoyed it. If you did, please consider leaving a review on the site where you purchased your copy. Reviews help readers like you discover new books, new contents and new ideas.